Family Circle

HOMETOWN COOKING.

Volume 8
Meredith. Consumer Marketing
Des Moines, Iowa

Family Circle₀ Hometown Cooking₀

Meredith₀ Consumer Marketing
Vice President, Consumer Marketing: Janet Donnelly
Consumer Marketing Product Director: Heather Sorensen
Consumer Marketing Product Manager: Wendy Merical
Consumer Marketing Billing/Renewal Manager: Tami Beachem
Business Director: Ron Clingman
Senior Production Manager: Al Rodruck

Waterbury Publications, Inc.
Editorial Director: Lisa Kingsley
Associate Editor: Tricia Bergman
Contributing Writer: Lisa Kingsley
Creative Director: Ken Carlson
Associate Design Director: Doug Samuelson
Graphic Designer: Mindy Samuelson
Contributing Copy Editors: Terri Fredrickson, Peg Smith
Contributing Indexer: Elizabeth T. Parson

Family Circle₀ **Magazine**
Editor in Chief: Linda Fears
Creative Director: Karmen Lizzul
Food Director: Regina Ragone, M.S., R.D.
Executive Food Editor: Julie Miltenberger
Associate Food Editor: Michael Tyrrell
Associate Food Editor: Melissa Knific
Editorial Assistant: Megan Bingham

Meredith National Media Group
President: Tom Harty

Meredith Corporation
Chairman and Chief Executive Officer: Stephen M. Lacy

In Memoriam: E.T. Meredith III (1933–2003)

All of us at Meredith₀ Consumer Marketing are dedicated to providing you with information and ideas to enhance your home. We welcome your comments and suggestions. Write to us at: Meredith Consumer Marketing, 1716 Locust St., Des Moines, IA 50309-3023.

Pictured on the front cover:
Rhubarb and Strawberry Coffee Cake
(recipe on page 167)
Photography by Jacob Fox

Enjoy prizewinning recipes from hometown America!

If you enjoy cooking—and competing—capturing first place in a recipe contest or winning a blue ribbon at a county or state fair is as good as it gets. Striving for perfection keeps competitive cooks working away in the kitchen, trying a little bit of this and a pinch of that. They make dishes again and again—testing them on family members, friends, and coworkers—until they get the result they're looking for. *Family Circle Hometown Cooking* is packed with just those kinds of recipes. Peruse its pages and sample the very best recipes from America's hometown cooks.

Included in the more than 140 recipes for special-occasion breakfasts, quick weeknight meals, healthy main dishes, and potluck favorites that will please a crowd is a decadent collection of everyone's favorite–desserts.

Along the way, you'll meet some of the cooks who contributed recipes to this book. Their stories make trying the recipe a richer experience. You'll learn a little about their recipes and about the cooks themselves—what inspires them, why they like to cook and bake, and who they love cooking for. When you taste their recipes, you'll know why they are winners—and maybe you'll be inspired to join their ranks.

— **The Editors**

table of
contents

CHAPTER 1
getting started

Celebrate with these nibbles and drinks for parties of any size and type.

STEEL YOUR HEART AWAY
EGGROLLS

DIPS AND SPREADS

Baked Mozzarella and Tomato-Basil Antipasti, 14

Jalapeño Crab and Corn Dip, 19

Tuscan White Bean Spread, 17

Vegetable Chili Con Queso, 16

NUTS AND SNACK MIX

Caesar Snack Mix, 19

Spicy Kettle Corn, 21

HOT APPETIZERS

Breezy Indian Spiced Chicken with Mango Peanut Sauce, Dates, and Grilled Mango, 11

Creamy Bacon-Filled Crescents, 8

Flatbread Pizza, 14

Goat Cheese and Fresh Mushroom Crostini, 13

Spicy Peking Chicken Wings, 13

Steel Your Heart Away Eggrolls, 23

COLD BEVERAGES

Pineapple-Ginger Punch, 24

Strawberry-Rhubarb Lemonade, 24

Creamy Bacon-Filled Crescents

These flaky spirals filled with cream cheese, Parmesan, bacon, and green onions are irresistible served warm. They are a nice substantial appetizer to serve when an array of snacks is dinner.

MAKES 16 servings   **PREP** 25 minutes   **BAKE** 12 minutes at 375°F

4	slices bacon, finely chopped
1	8-ounce package cream cheese, softened
½	cup freshly grated Parmesan cheese
2	to 4 green onions, thinly sliced (¼ cup)
1	tablespoon milk
2	8-ounce packages refrigerated crescent rolls (8 rolls each)
1	egg
1	tablespoon water
1	to 2 teaspoons poppy seeds
	Fresh chives (optional)

1 Preheat oven to 375°F. In a skillet cook bacon until crisp; drain. Line an extra large baking sheet with parchment paper; set aside. For filling, in a medium bowl stir together bacon, cream cheese, Parmesan cheese, green onions, and milk until nearly smooth; set aside.

2 Unroll and separate crescent rolls into 16 triangles. Spread each triangle with some of the cream cheese filling. Roll up from the wide end of the triangle. Place on prepared baking sheet.

3 In a small bowl beat egg with the water until combined. Brush crescents with the egg wash; sprinkle with poppy seeds.

4 Bake for 12 minutes or until puffed and light golden brown. If desired, garnish with chives. Serve warm.

Make-Ahead Directions Prepare as directed through Step 2. Cover and chill on prepared baking sheet up to 5 hours. (Or freeze in a single layer until firm. Place in a resealable plastic freezer bag and freeze up to 1 month. To bake, preheat oven to 375°F. Line a baking sheet with parchment paper. Arrange frozen filled crescents in a single layer on prepared baking sheet.) Bake crescents for 14 to 16 minutes or until golden and heated through.

PER SERVING 188 **CAL**; 13 g **FAT** (6 g **SAT**); 33 mg **CHOL**; 358 mg **SODIUM**; 12 g **CARB**; 0 g **FIBER**; 5 g **PRO**

Breezy Indian Spiced Chicken with Mango Peanut Sauce, Dates, and Grilled Mango

Naylet LaRochelle of Miami won the top prize of $25,000 in the sixth annual Dole® California Cook-Off with this Indian-inspired dish. She had to use at least one Dole packaged product and a Weber® gas grill to turn out something delicious in 60 minutes or less. Naylet has been fascinated with cooking since she was a girl. "I recall creating a make-believe kitchen in my backyard and pretending to make grand meals with the ingredients that my grandmother would give me," she says. "When the meal was done, I would bring it to my grandmother, who would always smile and lovingly say it was the best food she had ever tasted!"

MAKES 6 servings   **PREP** 20 minutes   **MARINATE** 15 minutes   **COOK** 5 minutes   **GRILL** 10 minutes

6	boneless, skinless chicken thighs
¾	cup hoisin sauce
1½	tablespoons lemon juice
1½	teaspoons grated fresh ginger
1¼	teaspoons garam masala
½	teaspoon kosher salt
3	cups DOLE® Frozen Mango Chunks, thawed
3	tablespoons peanut butter
2	tablespoons water
2	tablespoons Asian sweet chili sauce
2	teaspoons lemon juice
½	cup DOLE® California Chopped Dates
3	tablespoons snipped fresh cilantro

1 Place chicken in a resealable plastic bag set in a shallow dish; set aside. In a medium bowl combine ½ cup of the hoisin sauce, 1½ tablespoons lemon juice, the ginger, 1 teaspoon of the garam masala, and the kosher salt. Set aside about 3 tablespoons of marinade for grilling. Pour remaining marinade over chicken in bag. Seal bag; turn to coat chicken. Marinate in the refrigerator 15 minutes.

2 Meanwhile, place 2 cups of the mango chunks in a food processor or blender. Cover and process or blend until smooth.

3 In a medium saucepan combine mango puree, remaining ¼ cup hoisin sauce, the peanut butter, the water, and the remaining ¼ teaspoon garam masala. Cook over medium heat about 5 minutes or until smooth and heated through, stirring occasionally. Remove from heat. Stir in the sweet chili sauce and 2 teaspoons lemon juice; set aside. Thread remaining 1 cup mango chunks onto skewers*.

4 Drain chicken, discarding marinade. For a charcoal or gas grill, place chicken on the grill rack directly over medium heat. Cover and grill for 10 to 12 minutes or until chicken is no longer pink (180°F), turning once halfway through grilling and brushing once or twice with reserved marinade. Add mango kabobs to the grill for the last 1 to 2 minutes of grilling or until heated through.

5 To serve, place chicken on small plates and top with grilled mango. Sprinkle with dates and cilantro. Drizzle with mango sauce.

*Tip Soak wooden skewers in water for at least 30 minutes before using.

PER SERVING 353 **CAL**; 9 g **FAT** (2 g **SAT**); 108 mg **CHOL**; 730 mg **SODIUM**; 43 g **CARB**; 2 g **FIBER**; 26 g **PRO**

SPICY PEKING CHICKEN WINGS

Spicy Peking Chicken Wings

Sweet with a little heat, these glossy wings will be a hit at any gathering. Serve them with lots of napkins!

MAKES 12 servings   **PREP** 15 minutes   **COOK** 25 minutes

12	chicken wings (about 2½ pounds total)
2	tablespoons vegetable oil
½	cup dry white wine
½	cup plum sauce
⅓	cup reduced-sodium chicken broth
⅓	cup thinly sliced, peeled fresh ginger
2	tablespoons Asian chili-garlic sauce

1 Cut off and discard tips of chicken wings. Cut wings at joints to form 24 pieces. In an extra-large skillet heat oil over medium-high heat. Add chicken wings; cook for 10 minutes or until brown on both sides. Drain off fat.

2 For sauce, in a small bowl combine wine, plum sauce, broth, ginger, and chili-garlic sauce. Pour sauce over chicken wings. Bring to simmering. Cook, covered, for 5 minutes. Cook, uncovered, about 10 minutes more or until chicken is no longer pink and sauce is slightly thickened, stirring occasionally.

PER SERVING 171 **CAL**; 10 g **FAT** (3 g **SAT**); 39 mg **CHOL**; 236 mg **SODIUM**; 7 g **CARB**; 10 g **PRO**

Goat Cheese and Fresh Mushroom Crostini

These elegant cheese-topped toasts are delicious with a glass of chilled white wine or sparkling cider.

MAKES 30 servings   **PREP** 35 minutes
BAKE 7 minutes at 425°F/8 minutes at 375°

30	¼-inch slices baguette-style French bread
2	tablespoons olive oil
2	tablespoons butter
1½	cups coarsely chopped shallots or onions
8	ounces fresh cremini mushrooms, coarsely chopped (about 1½ cups)
1	tablespoon packed brown sugar
3	tablespoons balsamic vinegar
1	tablespoon snipped fresh thyme
¼	teaspoon salt
¼	teaspoon freshly ground black pepper
6	ounces soft goat cheese (chèvre)
2	tablespoons snipped fresh flat-leaf parsley (optional)

1 Preheat oven to 425°F. For crostini, arrange baguette slices on a large baking sheet. Lightly brush one side of slices with oil. Bake for 5 minutes. Turn slices over. Bake for 2 to 4 minutes more or until lightly browned. Set aside. Reduce oven temperature to 375°F.

2 Meanwhile, in a medium saucepan melt butter over medium-high heat. Add shallots; cook and stir for 3 minutes. Add mushrooms and brown sugar. Cook and stir for 1 minute. Stir in vinegar, thyme, salt, and pepper. Bring to boiling; reduce heat. Cook, uncovered, for 4 minutes or until most of the liquid is evaporated, stirring frequently.

3 Spread crostini with cheese. Bake for 8 minutes or until cheese is warm. Top with mushroom mixture. Drizzle with any remaining cooking liquid. If desired, sprinkle with parsley. Serve immediately.

PER SERVING 63 **CAL**; 3 g **FAT** (2 g **SAT**); 5 mg **CHOL**; 94 mg **SODIUM**; 6 g **CARB**; 2 g **PRO**

Baked Mozzarella and Tomato-Basil Antipasti

A jar of pasta sauce helps this warm and gooey dish go together in just 15 minutes. Pour the drinks while it bakes.

MAKES 4 servings   **PREP** 15 minutes
BAKE 20 minutes at 350°F   **BROIL** 3 minutes

2	cups pasta sauce
1	clove garlic, minced
8	ounces bite-size fresh mozzarella balls, or mozzarella cheese, cubed
1	tablespoon olive oil
¼	cup torn fresh basil leaves
1	baguette-style French bread, cut diagonally into ½-inch slices
	Olive oil
	Finely shredded Parmesan cheese
	Dried basil, crushed

1 Heat oven to 350°F. In four 12- to 16-ounce ovenproof dishes or one 1½-quart shallow ovenproof dish layer pasta sauce, garlic, and mozzarella. Bake for 20 minutes or until mozzarella is melted. Remove from oven; drizzle with the 1 tablespoon olive oil. Top with basil.

2 Lightly brush baguette slices with additional olive oil; place in a single layer on a large baking sheet. Broil 3 to 4 inches from the heat for 2 minutes. Turn slices; sprinkle lightly with shredded Parmesan and dried basil. Broil for 1 to 2 minutes more or until lightly toasted. Serve with baked mozzarella.

To Make Ahead Baguette slices can be broiled, cooled, and stored in an airtight container at room temperature up to 3 days.

PER SERVING 201 **CAL**; 10 g **FAT** (4 g **SAT**); 23 mg **CHOL**; 527 mg **SODIUM**; 17 g **CARB**; 1 g **FIBER**; 8 g **PRO**

Flatbread Pizza

If you prefer, use two 8-inch flatbreads in place of the cracker bread.

MAKES 12 servings   **PREP** 15 minutes
BAKE 8 minutes at 425°F

1	12- to 14-inch soft cracker bread (lavash)
1	recipe Quick Pizza Sauce or 1 cup pizza sauce
1	cup shredded pizza cheese (4 ounces)
½	cup sliced pepperoni or cooked sausage
½	cup sliced fresh mushrooms or chopped red sweet pepper
¼	cup sliced pitted ripe olives

1 Preheat oven to 425°F. Place cracker bread on an extra-large baking sheet. Spread Quick Pizza Sauce to within 1 inch of the edge. Sprinkle with cheese. Top with pepperoni, mushrooms, and olives.

2 Bake for 8 to 10 minutes or until cheese is melted and edge is lightly browned.

Quick Pizza Sauce In a small saucepan cook ½ cup chopped onion and 2 cloves minced garlic in 1 tablespoon hot oil over medium heat for 5 minutes or until onion is tender, stirring occasionally. Stir in one 8-ounce can tomato sauce; ½ teaspoon dried oregano, crushed; ½ teaspoon dried basil, crushed; ¼ teaspoon salt; and ¼ teaspoon crushed red pepper. Bring to boiling; reduce heat. Simmer, uncovered, about 5 minutes or until sauce reaches desired consistency.

PER SERVING 137 **CAL**; 7 g **FAT** (3 g **SAT**); 14 mg **CHOL**; 435 mg **SODIUM**; 12 g **CARB**; 1 g **FIBER**; 6 g **PRO**

FLATBREAD PIZZA

Vegetable Chili Con Queso

Prepare this hearty, cheesy vegetarian dip in a slow cooker—then keep it warm on low during the party.

MAKES 32 servings   **PREP** 20 minutes   **SLOW COOK** 6 hours (low) or 3 hours (high)

1	**15-ounce can pinto beans, rinsed and drained**
1	**15-ounce can black beans, rinsed and drained**
1	**15-ounce can chili beans with chili gravy, undrained**
1	**10-ounce can chopped tomatoes and green chile peppers, undrained**
1¼	**cups chopped zucchini (1 medium)**
1¼	**cups chopped yellow summer squash**
1	**cup chopped onion (1 large)**
¼	**cup tomato paste**
2	**to 3 teaspoons chili powder**
4	**cloves garlic, minced**
3	**cups shredded Colby and Monterey Jack cheese (12 ounces)**
	Tortilla or corn chips

1 In a 3½- or 4-quart slow cooker combine pinto beans, black beans, chili beans with chili gravy, tomatoes and green chile peppers, zucchini, summer squash, onion, tomato paste, chili powder, and garlic.

2 Cover and cook on low-heat setting for 6 to 7 hours or on high-heat setting for 3 to 3½ hours. Stir in cheese until melted. Serve immediately or keep warm, covered, on warm setting or low-heat setting up to 1 hour.

3 Serve dip with tortilla chips.

PER SERVING 81 **CAL**; 4 g **FAT** (2 g **SAT**); 9 mg **CHOL**; 231 mg **SODIUM**; 8 g **CARB**; 2 g **FIBER**; 5 g **PRO**

Tuscan White Bean Spread

If you have any leftovers, tuck this creamy, garlicky dip into a pita half with your favorite cheese and lots of fresh veggies for a satisfying and portable lunch.

MAKES 18 servings **PREP** 15 minutes **CHILL** 2 hours

2	**15-ounce cans great Northern beans or cannellini beans (white kidney beans), rinsed and drained**
½	**cup chicken broth or vegetable broth**
1	**tablespoon olive oil**
3	**cloves garlic, minced**
1	**teaspoon snipped fresh thyme and/or fresh rosemary**
⅛	**teaspoon crushed red pepper**
	Olive oil (optional)
	Fresh thyme leaves and/or snipped fresh rosemary (optional)
1	**recipe Baked Pita Chips or purchased pita chips (optional)**
	Sweet pepper strips or carrot sticks (optional)

1 In a food processor* combine beans, broth, the 1 tablespoon oil, the garlic, the 1 teaspoon thyme and/or rosemary, and the crushed red pepper. Cover and process until nearly smooth. Transfer spread to a serving bowl. Cover and chill for 2 to 24 hours.

2 Serve bean spread chilled or at room temperature. If desired, drizzle spread with additional oil, sprinkle with additional thyme and/or rosemary, and serve with pita chips and/or sweet pepper strips or carrot sticks.

*If you don't have a food processor, in a large bowl combine the beans, broth, the 1 tablespoon oil, the garlic, the 1 teaspoon thyme and/or rosemary, and the crushed red pepper. Using a potato masher, mash bean mixture until spread reaches desired consistency. Continue as directed.

PER SERVING 57 **CAL**; 1 g **FAT** (0 g **SAT**); 0 mg **CHOL**; 26 mg **SODIUM**; 9 g **CARB**; 2 g **FIBER**; 3 g **PRO**

Baked Pita Chips Preheat oven to 350°F. Split 2 pita bread rounds in half horizontally; cut each pita half into six wedges. Place pita wedges in a single layer on a large baking sheet. In a small bowl combine 2 tablespoons olive oil and ¼ teaspoon kosher salt. Brush pita wedges with oil mixture. Bake for 12 to 15 minutes or until crisp and lightly browned. Remove from baking sheet and cool on a wire rack. Makes 24 chips.

JALAPEÑO CRAB AND CORN DIP

Jalapeño Crab and Corn Dip

Look for backfin crabmeat to make this recipe. Backfin, which is reasonably priced, has enough texture to be attractive and detectable in the dip.

MAKES 28 servings   **PREP** 30 minutes
BAKE 15 minutes at 425°F

2	tablespoons butter
1	cup frozen whole kernel corn
½	cup chopped red sweet pepper (1 small)
1	clove garlic, minced
½	cup sour cream
½	cup mayonnaise
½	cup sliced pickled jalapeño chile peppers, drained and chopped
1	teaspoon Worcestershire sauce
1	teaspoon bottled hot pepper sauce (optional)
2	6- to 6.5-ounce cans crabmeat, drained, flaked, and cartilage removed
1	cup shredded Monterey Jack cheese (4 ounces)
2	tablespoons grated Parmesan cheese
	Tortilla chips

1 Preheat oven to 425°F. In a seasoned or generously greased 8- to 9-inch cast-iron skillet melt butter over medium heat. Add corn, sweet pepper, and garlic; cook for 5 minutes or until tender.

2 In a medium bowl combine sour cream, mayonnaise, jalapeños, Worcestershire sauce, and, if desired, hot pepper sauce. Stir in corn mixture, crabmeat, and Monterey Jack cheese. Transfer dip to the same cast-iron skillet.

3 Sprinkle dip with Parmesan cheese. Bake for 15 minutes or until golden and bubbly around the edge. Serve with tortilla chips.

PER SERVING 74 **CAL**; 6 g **FAT** (2 g **SAT**); 20 mg **CHOL**; 124 mg **SODIUM**; 2 g **CARB**; 3 g **PRO**

Slow Cooker Directions Prepare as directed through Step 2, using any large skillet to cook corn mixture. After transferring crab mixture to the same large skillet, heat through over low heat. Transfer dip to a greased 1½-quart slow cooker. Cover and cook on low-heat setting for 1½ to 2 hours or until bubbly. Sprinkle with Parmesan cheese. Serve with tortilla chips.

Caesar Snack Mix

Take a break from Ranch! This savory jumble of pita chips, cereals, almonds and pecans is flavored with lemony, garlicky Caesar dressing, Parmesan cheese, and a hit of hot sauce.

MAKES 22 servings   **PREP** 25 minutes
BAKE 45 minutes at 250°F

1	6- to 9-ounce package plain pita chips
4	cups round toasted oat cereal
4	cups bite-size rice square cereal
4	cups bite-size corn square cereal
1½	cups whole almonds
1½	cups pecan halves
2	tablespoons dried parsley flakes
1	cup butter
½	cup grated Parmesan cheese
¼	cup bottled Caesar salad dressing (not creamy)
1	teaspoon garlic powder
	Several drops bottled hot pepper sauce

1 Preheat oven to 250°F. In a roasting pan combine pita chips, oat cereal, rice cereal, corn cereal, almonds, pecans, and parsley; set aside.

2 In a small saucepan combine butter, cheese, Caesar dressing, garlic powder, and hot pepper sauce. Stir over medium heat until butter is melted. Drizzle butter mixture over cereal mixture; stir gently to coat.

3 Bake for 45 minutes, stirring every 15 minutes. Spread snack mix on a large sheet of foil to cool. Store in an airtight container at room temperature up to 2 weeks or freeze up to 3 months.

PER SERVING 289 **CAL**; 22 g **FAT** (7 g **SAT**); 24 mg **CHOL**; 331 mg **SODIUM**; 21 g **CARB**; 3 g **FIBER**; 6 g **PRO**

Spicy Kettle Corn

Marianne Carlson of Jefferson, Iowa, grew up eating her grandmother's "sugar corn" (more commonly called "kettle corn" these days). The tradition was passed along to her father—who made it to take to the nursing home and to church—and then to Marianne. A long-time Iowa State Fair recipe contest entrant, Marianne decided to spice things up with chipotle chile powder, cardamom, and cinnamon for the 2014 "My Favorite Tone's Spice" contest in the Casual Appetizers category. She won bragging rights and $2,000 for her sweet, spicy, and salty snack.

MAKES 10 servings   **START TO FINISH** 20 minutes

½   **cup sugar**
½   **teaspoon Spice Islands® Chipotle Chile Powder**
½   **teaspoon Spice Islands® Ground Cardamom**
¼   **teaspoon Spice Islands® Ground Saigon Cinnamon**
⅓   **cup Mazola® Corn Oil**
½   **cup unpopped popcorn**
     Spice Islands® Fine Grind Sea Salt

1 In a small bowl combine sugar, chile powder, cardamom, and cinnamon. Set aside.

2 Place oil in a stove top popcorn popper*. Heat over medium-high heat. Add popcorn and sugar mixture to hot oil. Pop for 10 minutes, stirring constantly (using the crank handle on the popper) or until all popcorn has popped. Spread on a large foil-lined baking sheet. Season to taste with salt. Cool completely.

3 Pour into a large serving bowl. Store leftovers in a tightly closed container.

* Use a popper with an internal stirring mechanism to prevent the sugar from burning and evenly distribute the coating over all kernels.

PER SERVING 137 **CAL**; 8 g **FAT** (1 g **SAT**); 110 mg **SODIUM**; 18 g **CARB**; 2 g **FIBER**; 1 g **PRO**

Steel Your Heart Away Eggrolls

Sometimes a recipe is just so crazily creative, it upends expectations in the best way possible. That was the case for Fort Worth, Texas, cook Paula Todora, who won the Bob's Red Mill® 2013 Spar for the Spurtle contest with these crispy eggrolls stuffed with a coconut milk-infused filling of steel cut oats, apples, nuts, and spices. The prize was a trip for two to Scotland plus $2,500 spending money so she could represent Bob's Red Mill® in the Golden Spurtle contest. What's a spurtle? An ancient Scottish wooden dowel-shape tool used for stirring oatmeal and soups.

MAKES 12 servings **PREP** 30 minutes **CHILL** overnight **COOK** 22 minutes **FRY** 3 minutes per batch

1   **cup Bob's Red Mill® Steel Cut Oats**
1   **cup unsweetened coconut milk**
¾   **cup water**
2   **large Granny Smith apples, peeled, cored, and chopped**
¾   **cup packed brown sugar**
3   **tablespoons lemon juice**
2   **tablespoons pure maple syrup**
1   **teaspoon ground cinnamon**
¼   **teaspoon sea salt**
⅛   **teaspoon ground nutmeg**
⅛   **teaspoon ground cloves**
½   **cup coarsely chopped walnuts**
½   **cup golden raisins**
12   **eggroll wrappers**
     Peanut or vegetable oil
¾   **cup orange marmalade**
2   **tablespoons honey**
¼   **cup powdered sugar**

1 In a small bowl combine oats, coconut milk, and the water. Cover and soak in the refrigerator overnight.

2 In a large saucepan combine soaked oats, apples, brown sugar, lemon juice, maple syrup, cinnamon, salt, nutmeg, and cloves. Bring to boiling. Reduce heat and simmer 10 minutes, stirring occasionally.

3 Add walnuts and raisins. Simmer, covered, 12 to 14 minutes or until apples and oats are tender, stirring occasionally. Quickly cool mixture by placing saucepan in a large bowl of ice water, stirring constantly.

4 With a corner of an eggroll wrapper toward you, place ¼ cup filling across the center and spread from side to side, leaving a 1-inch border on each side. Fold the bottom corner up and over the filling. Fold in sides. Brush edges of top corner with water; roll up to seal. Repeat with remaining eggroll wrappers and filling.

5 In a large heavy pot or Dutch oven heat 3 inches of oil to 365°F. Fry 3 eggrolls at a time in hot oil for 3 to 4 minutes or until golden, turning once. Remove with tongs and drain on paper towels.

6 In a small bowl combine orange marmalade and honey. To serve, cut each eggroll in half diagonally; dust with powdered sugar. Serve warm with dipping sauce.

PER SERVING 458 **CAL**; 17 g **FAT** (5 g **SAT**); 3 mg **CHOL**; 256 mg **SODIUM**; 74 g **CARB**; 4 g **FIBER**; 6 g **PRO**

Pineapple-Ginger Punch

Refreshing and not overly sweet, this bright flavor punch is lovely for graduation parties and baby and wedding showers—or at casual backyard barbecues.

MAKES 8 servings   **PREP** 20 minutes   **COOL** 1 hour
CHILL 2 hours

- 1   **cup water**
- ½   **cup sugar**
- ⅔   **cup thinly sliced unpeeled fresh ginger (about 4 ounces)**
- 2½   **cups unsweetened pineapple juice, chilled**
- 3   **tablespoons lemon juice**
- 3   **tablespoons lime juice**
- 1   **1-liter club soda, chilled**
      Ice cubes
      Lime slices and/or pineapple wedges

1 In a small saucepan combine the water, sugar, and ginger. Bring to boiling, stirring until sugar is dissolved; reduce heat. Simmer, uncovered, for 10 minutes. Cool ginger mixture to room temperature. Strain ginger mixture through a fine-mesh sieve into a bowl. Cover with plastic wrap; chill for at least 2 hours.

2 In a large punch bowl or pitcher combine the chilled ginger mixture, pineapple juice, lemon juice, and lime juice. Stir in club soda. Add ice cubes and lime slices and/or pineapple wedges.

PER SERVING 102 **CAL**; 0 g **FAT** (0 g **SAT**); 0 mg **CHOL**; 30 mg **SODIUM**; 26 g **CARB**; 1 g **FIBER**; 1 g **PRO**

Strawberry-Rhubarb Lemonade

Make this pretty-in-pink drink in late spring and early summer when rhubarb and strawberries are in season.

MAKES 6 servings   **PREP** 15 minutes   **COOL** 50 minutes
CHILL 2 hours

- 4   **cups cold water**
- 2½   **cups chopped fresh rhubarb (about 12 ounces)**
- 1¼   **cups sugar**
- 1   **tablespoon finely shredded lemon peel**
- 2   **cups quartered fresh strawberries**
- 1   **cup lemon juice**
- 1   **teaspoon vanilla**
- 1   **cup sparkling water or carbonated water, chilled (optional)**
      Ice cubes
      Lemon slices (optional)
      Fresh strawberries (optional)

1 In a large saucepan combine the 4 cups water, rhubarb, sugar, and lemon peel. Bring to boiling; reduce heat, stirring until sugar is dissolved. Simmer, covered, for 10 minutes. Remove from heat. Stir in 1 cup of the quartered strawberries. Cool for 20 minutes.

2 Pour mixture through a fine-mesh sieve into a large pitcher. Press fruit pulp with the back of a spoon to extract as much juice as possible; discard pulp. Stir lemon juice and vanilla into juice mixture. Cool for 30 minutes. Cover and chill for 2 to 24 hours.

3 To serve, add the remaining 1 cup quartered strawberries and, if desired, sparkling water to lemonade in the pitcher. Serve lemonade in glasses over ice cubes. If desired, garnish with lemon slices and additional strawberries.

PER SERVING 201 **CAL**; 0 g **FAT** (0 g **SAT**); 0 mg **CHOL**; 8 mg **SODIUM**; 52 g **CARB**; 2 g **FIBER**; 1 g **PRO**

STRAWBERRY-RHUBARB LEMONADE

CHAPTER 2
bring on breakfast

Brighten the beginning of the day with something good to eat.

SATURDAY CINNAMON ROLLS

EGG AND CHEESE DISHES

Baked Eggs with Cheese and Basil Sauce, 30

Sausage and Egg Po'Boys, 31

Sausage-Pepper Frittata, 29

Spicy Breakfast Tacos, 35

Sweet Potato Biscuit Sandwiches with
Ham and Redeye Gravy, 32

BREAKFAST BREADS AND CEREALS

Apple-Streusel Muffins, 45

Bacon and Apple Waffles, 36

Berry Breakfast Pizzas, 41

Blueberry Brie Stuffed French Toast With Blueberry
Rosemary Syrup, 39

Buttermilk Bran Pancakes, 37

Fruit Muesli, 47

Saturday Cinnamon Rolls, 42

Sweet Dutch Baby, 40

Zucchini-Chocolate Chip Scones, 46

Sausage-Pepper Frittata

Part of what makes this the winning dish from the 2014 Iowa Egg Council Incredibly Good Eggs contest is the bread used in it. Carol Chase of Sioux City, Iowa, had warm memories of making bread with her mother. She started baking bread with fresh-milled wheat flour from a local farm—then learned about sponge baking from a European baking book a friend gave to her. She used her own whole-wheat sponge bread as a base, then combined it with eggs, sausage, cheese, and lots of vegetables—and she had a winner on her hands.

MAKES 8 servings   **PREP** 25 minutes   **COOK** 20 minutes   **BAKE** 45 minutes at 325°F

	Nonstick cooking spray
3	tablespoons olive oil
4	red, green, orange, and/or yellow sweet peppers, cut into thin strips
1	large onion, thinly sliced
3	cloves garlic, minced
3	small yellow summer squash and/or zucchini, thinly sliced
8	ounces fresh mushrooms, sliced
1	pound bulk pork sausage
6	eggs, lightly beaten
¼	cup milk
8	slices whole wheat bread, cubed
2	cups shredded Swiss cheese
1	8-ounce package cream cheese, cut into cubes

1 Preheat oven to 325°F. Lightly coat a 3-quart baking dish with nonstick cooking spray; set aside.

2 In a large skillet cook peppers, onion, and garlic in 1 tablespoon hot oil over medium heat for 5 minutes or until tender. Remove from skillet; set aside. Add 1 tablespoon oil to the skillet. Cook squash for 5 minutes or until golden and tender. Remove from skillet; set aside. Add 1 tablespoon oil to the skillet. Cook mushrooms for 5 minutes or until golden and tender. Transfer to paper towels; set aside.

3 In the same skillet cook sausage over medium heat until browned, stirring occasionally. Drain off fat; set aside.

4 In a large bowl combine eggs and milk. Add reserved vegetables, half the bread cubes, Swiss cheese, and cream cheese; stir gently to combine.

5 Transfer remaining bread cubes to the prepared dish. Spoon 1½ cups of vegetable mixture into the dish. Top with sausage and remaining vegetable mixture. Bake for 45 minutes or until a knife inserted in the center comes out clean. Serve warm.

PER SERVING 616 **CAL**; 46 g **FAT** (19 g **SAT**); 242 mg **CHOL**; 678 mg **SODIUM**; 22 g **CARB**; 4 g **FIBER**; 30 g **PRO**

Baked Eggs with Cheese and Basil Sauce

Creamy baked eggs flavored with basil and served in individual casseroles—with toast for dipping—are an elegant dish to serve at a celebratory brunch.

MAKES 4 servings   **PREP** 15 minutes   **BAKE** 18 minutes at 350°F

3	**tablespoons butter**
2	**tablespoons all-purpose flour**
¼	**teaspoon salt**
⅛	**teaspoon black pepper**
3	**tablespoons snipped fresh basil or ½ teaspoon dried basil, crushed**
1	**cup fat-free milk**
	Nonstick cooking spray
4	**eggs**
	Salt
	Black pepper
¼	**cup reduced-fat shredded mozzarella cheese (1 ounce)**
	Snipped fresh basil (optional)
	Toasted bread slices (optional)

1 Preheat oven to 350°F. For sauce, in a small saucepan melt butter over medium heat. Stir in flour, the ¼ teaspoon salt, and the ⅛ teaspoon pepper. Stir in dried basil (if using). Add milk all at once. Cook and stir until thickened and bubbly; cook and stir for 1 minute more. Remove from heat. Stir in the 3 tablespoons fresh basil (if using).

2 Lightly coat four 8- to 10-ounce round baking dishes or 6-ounce custard cups with cooking spray. Spoon about 2 tablespoons of the sauce into each prepared baking dish. Gently break an egg into the center of each dish; sprinkle with additional salt and pepper. Spoon the remaining sauce over eggs.

3 Bake for 18 to 20 minutes or until eggs are set. Sprinkle with cheese. Let stand until cheese is melted. If desired, sprinkle with additional basil and serve with toasted bread.

PER SERVING 204 **CAL**; 15 g **FAT** (8 g **SAT**); 213 mg **CHOL**; 441 mg **SODIUM**; 7 g **CARB**; 11 g **PRO**

Sausage and Egg Po'Boys

A New Orleans classic gets a morning makeover with hard-cooked eggs and savory sage-infused breakfast sausage, all tucked into a hoagie bun with crisp lettuce and a rich remoulade sauce.

MAKES 4 servings   **START TO FINISH** 25 minutes

½   **cup Spicy Remoulade**
1   **pound bulk breakfast sausage**
2   **teaspoons Dijon mustard**
     Nonstick cooking spray
4   **hoagie buns, split**
     Shredded iceberg lettuce
8   **lengthwise sandwich pickle slices (optional)**
4   **hard-cooked eggs, sliced**
     Bottled hot pepper sauce (optional)

1 Prepare Spicy Remoulade. Set aside.

2 In a medium bowl combine sausage and mustard. Shape mixture into six 4-inch-diameter patties. Coat a large nonstick skillet with cooking spray; heat skillet over medium-high heat. Add patties; cook about 6 minutes or until no longer pink, turning once. Remove from skillet. Cut patties into ½-inch strips.

3 Spread the bottoms of hoagie buns with some of the Spicy Remoulade. Layer with lettuce, sausage strips, pickle slices (if desired), and hard-cooked eggs. Drizzle with the remaining Spicy Remoulade and, if desired, sprinkle with hot pepper sauce.

Spicy Remoulade In a medium bowl combine 1 cup mayonnaise, ¼ cup pickle relish, 2 tablespoons drained capers, 1 tablespoon Creole or spicy brown mustard, 1 tablespoon snipped fresh parsley, 2 teaspoons bottled hot pepper sauce, and 1 teaspoon fresh lemon juice. Makes 1¼ cups.

PER SERVING 757 **CAL**; 52 g **FAT** (15 g **SAT**); 274 mg **CHOL**; 1,294 mg **SODIUM**; 41 g **CARB**; 2 g **FIBER**; 32 g **PRO**

Sweet Potato Biscuit Sandwiches with Ham and Redeye Gravy

Southern-style redeye gravy is made with the drippings from pan-fried bacon, sausage, or ham stirred together with coffee. Although some believe the "red eye" references the coffee that will keep a person awake, there is another explanation for its name. When poured into a bowl, the coffee sinks to the bottom and the drippings float to the top, creating the appearance of a "red eye."

MAKES 4 servings   **PREP** 45 minutes   **BAKE** 12 minutes at 450°F   **COOK** 15 minutes

3	cups all-purpose flour
1	tablespoon baking powder
1	tablespoon sugar
1	teaspoon salt
¾	teaspoon cream of tartar
¼	teaspoon cayenne pepper
⅓	cup butter
1	cup shredded cheddar cheese
1	cup milk
½	cup mashed cooked sweet potato
4	slices bacon
1	¼-inch thick fully cooked ham slice (about 5 oz.), cut into 4 equal pieces
1	cup strong coffee
¼	cup peach preserves
4	eggs, scrambled
	Fresh flat-leaf parsley leaves

1 Preheat oven to 450°F. For sweet potato biscuits, in a large bowl combine flour, baking powder, sugar, salt, cream of tartar, and cayenne pepper. Using a pastry blender, cut in butter until mixture resembles coarse crumbs. Stir in cheese. Make a well in the center of the flour mixture. In a small bowl combine milk and sweet potato. Add sweet potato mixture to flour mixture. Using a fork, stir just until dough is moistened.

2 Turn out dough onto a well-floured surface. Knead gently 10 to 12 strokes. Pat or lightly roll dough to a ¾-inch thick rectangle (about 9×5 inches). Cut into eight pieces. Place biscuits 1 inch apart on a large baking sheet. Bake for 12 to 14 minutes or until lightly browned.*

3 Meanwhile, in a large skillet cook bacon until crisp. Drain on paper towels, reserving 1 tablespoon bacon fat in the skillet. Add ham to skillet; cook for 5 minutes or until well browned on both sides. Add coffee to skillet with ham, stirring to scrape up any browned bits. Simmer, uncovered, until coffee just begins to thicken and glazes the ham. Remove ham from skillet.

4 Split biscuits. Top bottoms with ham, peach preserves, scrambled eggs, bacon, parsley, and biscuit tops.

*This recipe uses four of the eight biscuits. Bake and cool completely, then wrap and freeze any leftover biscuits for another use. To reheat, thaw biscuits and wrap in foil. Bake at 350°F for 10 minutes.

PER SERVING 595 **CAL**; 28 g **FAT** (14 g **SAT**); 261 mg **CHOL**; 1,398 mg **SODIUM**; 60 g **CARB**; 3 g **FIBER**; 26 g **PRO**

Spicy Breakfast Tacos

After four years living and traveling in Mexico with his wife, Jillian, Malcolm Bedell says that nearly all of their meals were folded into fresh, handmade, still-warm tortillas—and breakfast was no exception. That, he says, is what he wanted to bring to this prizewinning recipe from the 2013 Rise, Sizzle, and Shine recipe contest sponsored by Jones Dairy Farm. Malcolm and Jillian write about food from Rockland, Maine, on their blog, fromaway.com. They plan to use the $2,000 prize money toward opening a sandwich shop in Malcolm's hometown. "We don't have quite enough money yet," he says, "but we're getting closer."

MAKES 6 servings   **START TO FINISH** 20 minutes

1	teaspoon vegetable oil
1	12-ounce package Jones Dairy Farm® All Natural Pork Sausage Roll
8	eggs
5	tablespoons water
	Salt and black pepper
1	tablespoon butter
1	cup shredded Mexican-style four cheese blend
12	6-inch corn tortillas, warmed*
1	medium tomato, diced
¼	cup Mexican crema or sour cream
3	green onions, thinly sliced
2	tablespoons grated Cotija or Parmesan cheese
	Hot sauce

1 In a large skillet heat vegetable oil over medium-high heat. Add sausage and cook about 10 minutes, stirring occasionally, until browned and crunchy. Remove with slotted spoon and drain on a paper towel-lined plate; set aside. Wipe skillet clean with a paper towel.

2 For the scrambled eggs, in medium bowl whisk together eggs, the water, salt, and pepper. In the same skillet melt butter over medium heat; pour in eggs. Cook over medium heat, without stirring, until eggs begins to set on the bottom and around edges. With a spatula or large spoon, lift and fold the partially cooked eggs so the uncooked portion flows underneath. Continue cooking over medium heat for 2 to 3 minutes or until eggs are cooked through but are still glossy and moist. Stir in sausage and Mexican blend cheese. Immediately remove skillet from heat.

3 To assemble tacos, place one-fourth of the scrambled eggs on each tortilla . Top with tomato, crema, green onions, and sprinkle with Cotija. Serve with hot sauce.

* Stack the tortillas and wrap in foil. Warm in a 350°F oven for 10 minutes before serving.

PER SERVING 471 **CAL**; 33 g **FAT** (13 g **SAT**); 322 mg **CHOL**; 749 mg **SODIUM**; 18 g **CARB**; 3 g **FIBER**; 25 g **PRO**

Bacon and Apple Waffles

These waffles get a double dose of bacon and apples—in the batter and on top. The result is bite after airy bite of sweet, salty, smoky flavor.

MAKES 12 servings **PREP** 15 minutes **BAKE** per waffle baker directions

1¾	**cups all-purpose flour**
2	**tablespoons sugar**
1	**tablespoon baking powder**
¼	**teaspoon salt**
2	**eggs, lightly beaten**
1¾	**cups milk**
½	**cup vegetable oil or butter, melted**
1	**teaspoon vanilla**
½	**cup crumbled, crisp-cooked bacon**
¼	**cup chopped apple**
⅔	**cup coarsely chopped apple (1 medium) (optional)**
3	**slices crumbled, crisp-cooked bacon (optional) Syrup (optional)**

1 In a large bowl stir together flour, sugar, baking powder, and salt. Make a well in the center of flour mixture; set aside.

2 In a medium bowl combine eggs, milk, oil, and vanilla. Add egg mixture all at once to flour mixture. Stir just until moistened (batter should be slightly lumpy). Stir in the ½ cup crumbled bacon and the ¼ cup chopped apple.

3 Add batter to a preheated, lightly greased waffle baker according to the manufacturer's directions (use a regular or Belgian waffle baker). Close lid quickly; do not open until done. Bake according to the manufacturer's directions. When done, use a fork to lift waffle off grid. Repeat with the remaining batter. Serve warm. If desired, top with the coarsely chopped apple and crumbled bacon. Serve with syrup.

PER SERVING 216 **CAL**; 13 g **FAT** (2 g **SAT**); 40 mg **CHOL**; 291 mg **SODIUM**; 19 g **CARB**; 1 g **FIBER**; 6 g **PRO**

Buttermilk Bran Pancakes

Buttermilk gives these whole-grain pancakes light, fluffy texture and tangy taste, which is delicious paired with the sweetness of maple syrup and fresh fruit.

MAKES 12 servings   **START TO FINISH** 25 minutes

1½   **cups all-purpose flour**
¼   **cup wheat bran**
2   **tablespoons granulated sugar**
2   **teaspoons baking powder**
½   **teaspoon baking soda**
¼   **teaspoon salt**
1   **egg, lightly beaten**
1½   **cups buttermilk or sour milk***
3   **tablespoons canola oil**
   Fresh fruit (optional)**
   Syrup, warmed if desired (optional)

1 In a large bowl stir together flour, wheat bran, sugar, baking powder, baking soda, and salt. In another bowl use a fork to combine egg, buttermilk, and oil. Add egg mixture all at once to flour mixture. Stir just until moistened (batter should be slightly lumpy). If desired, stir in fruit.

2 For dollar-size pancakes, pour about 1 tablespoon batter onto a hot, lightly greased griddle or heavy skillet. Spread batter, if necessary. Cook over medium heat for 1 to 2 minutes on each side or until pancakes are golden brown; turn over when surfaces are bubbly and edges are slightly dry. Serve warm. If desired, top with fresh fruit and syrup.

*Tip For sour milk, place 4½ teaspoons lemon juice or vinegar in a 2-cup glass measuring cup. Add enough milk to equal 1½ cups. Let stand for 5 minutes before using.

**Fruit Options Stir one of the following fruits into the pancake batter before pouring portions onto griddle: ½ cup chopped fresh apple, apricot, peach, nectarine, or pear; ½ cup fresh or frozen blueberries; or ¼ cup chopped dried apple, pear, apricot, raisins, currants, dates, cranberries, blueberries, cherries, or mixed fruit.

PER SERVING 116 **CAL**; 4 g **FAT** (1 g **SAT**); 17 mg **CHOL**; 221 mg **SODIUM**; 17 g **CARB**; 1 g **FIBER**; 3 g **PRO**

Buttermilk Pancakes Prepare as directed, except use 1¾ cups all-purpose flour and omit wheat bran.

Whole Wheat Pancakes Prepare as directed, except use 1¾ cups whole wheat flour in place of the all-purpose flour, omit wheat bran, and substitute packed brown sugar for the granulated sugar.

Blueberry Brie Stuffed French Toast with Blueberry Rosemary Syrup

Sweet and savory breakfasts are the specialty of Lauren Wyler of Dripping Springs, Texas. She took top honors at the 2014 Our State's Magazine Blueberry Recipe Contest, co-sponsored by the North Carolina Blueberry Council, with her recipe that combines buttery brie and pine-scented rosemary with sweet-tart blueberries. "It's rich, it looks stunning, and the payoff is a great dish you didn't have to slave over," says Lauren.

MAKES 4 servings   **PREP** 30 minutes   **COOK** 20 minutes

1¾ **cups fresh blueberries**
1   **cup pure maple syrup**
¼   **cup orange juice**
¼   **cup sugar**
1   **sprig fresh rosemary**
4   **1½-inch-thick slices Hawaiian Bread or challah**
4   **ounces brie, rind removed, and cut into small cubes**
2   **eggs**
¼   **cup whole milk**
1   **teaspoon pure vanilla extract**
1   **tablespoon butter**

1 For the Blueberry Rosemary Syrup, in a medium saucepan combine 1½ cups of the blueberries, the maple syrup, orange juice, sugar, and rosemary sprig. Bring to boiling, stirring to dissolve sugar. Reduce heat; simmer, uncovered, 15 minutes or until blueberries burst and syrup becomes slightly thickened (watch pan carefully and adjust heat as needed so syrup does not boil over).

2 While the syrup is simmering, prepare the French toast. Using a small sharp paring knife, cut a pocket in the bread slices, being careful not to cut all the way through the bread slices. Place 1 ounce of brie and about 1 tablespoon of the remaining blueberries in the pocket of each bread slice.

3 In a shallow dish whisk together the eggs, milk, and vanilla.

4 In a large nonstick skillet melt the butter over medium-low heat. Dip each piece of stuffed French toast into the egg and milk mixture and place in the skillet. Cook the French toast for 2 to 3 minutes per side or until lightly browned.

5 Remove the syrup from the heat; discard the rosemary sprig. Serve immediately with the stuffed French toast slices*.

*Place remaining blueberry syrup in an airtight container. Refrigerate up to 1 week. Serve on pancakes, waffles, ice cream, or cheesecake.

PER SERVING 621 **CAL**; 18 g **FAT** (10 g **SAT**); 154 mg **CHOL**; 381 mg **SODIUM**; 102 g **CARB**; 3 g **FIBER**; 16 g **PRO**

Sweet Dutch Baby

Dutch oven pancakes puff magically in the oven, then deflate rather quickly when removed from the heat. Call everyone to the table to catch the impressive sight before it sinks! No matter how fluffy or flat, however, the flavor is wonderful.

MAKES 6 servings   **PREP** 25 minutes   **STAND** 30 minutes   **BAKE** 25 minutes at 425°F

3	eggs
½	cup milk
3	tablespoons granulated sugar
¾	teaspoon ground cinnamon
1	cup thinly sliced Braeburn apple (1 medium)
2	tablespoons butter, cut up
½	cup all-purpose flour
½	teaspoon vanilla
⅛	teaspoon salt
	Powdered sugar

1 Allow eggs and milk to stand at room temperature for 30 minutes. Meanwhile, preheat oven to 425°F.

2 In a small bowl stir together 2 tablespoons of the granulated sugar and ¼ teaspoon of the cinnamon. Add apple slices; toss until well coated.

3 Place butter in a 9- to 10-inch oven-proof skillet. Heat skillet in oven for 2 minutes or until butter is melted. Remove skillet from oven; swirl skillet to coat surface.

4 Spread apple slices evenly in skillet. Bake for 10 minutes or until apples have softened slightly and butter is bubbling and beginning to brown around the edges.

5 Meanwhile, for pancake batter, in a blender combine eggs, milk, flour, vanilla, salt, the remaining granulated sugar, and the remaining cinnamon. Cover and blend for 1 minute or until well mixed and frothy.

6 Remove skillet from oven. Evenly pour batter over apples. Bake for 25 to 30 minutes or until puffy and golden brown. Cool slightly in skillet on a wire rack. (The Dutch Baby will deflate quite a bit.) Dust with powdered sugar. Cut into wedges.

PER SERVING 160 **CAL**; 7 g **FAT** (3 g **SAT**); 105 mg **CHOL**; 128 mg **SODIUM**; 20 g **CARB**; 1 g **FIBER**; 5 g **PRO**

Berry Breakfast Pizzas

Sweetened cream cheese with cardamom and orange stirred in is the "sauce" on these fresh-berry breakfast pies.

MAKES 4 servings   **START TO FINISH** 25 minutes

¼   **cup granulated sugar**
4   **teaspoons cornstarch**
    Dash salt
½   **cup water**
2   **cups mixed fresh berries, such as blueberries, raspberries, and/or blackberries**
1   **teaspoon butter**
1   **teaspoon finely shredded orange peel**
4   **ounces reduced-fat cream cheese (Neufchâtel), softened**
2   **tablespoons orange marmalade**
2   **teaspoons granulated sugar**
¼   **teaspoon ground cardamom**
2   **pita bread rounds, split horizontally and toasted**
2   **tablespoons butter, melted**
    Powdered sugar (optional)

1 For berry topping, in a medium saucepan stir together the ¼ cup granulated sugar, the cornstarch, and salt. Stir in the water. Stir in ½ cup of the berries. Cook and stir over medium heat until thickened. Remove from heat. Add 1 cup of the berries and the 1 teaspoon butter, stirring until butter is melted. Gently stir in orange peel.

2 In a medium mixing bowl beat cream cheese and orange marmalade with a mixer on low to medium until smooth. In a small bowl stir together the 2 teaspoons granulated sugar and the cardamom.

3 Brush cut sides of pita rounds with the 2 tablespoons melted butter; sprinkle with the sugar-cardamom mixture. Spread cream cheese mixture and berry topping over pita rounds. Top with the remaining berries. If desired, sprinkle with powdered sugar.

PER SERVING 343 **CAL**; 14 g **FAT** (8 g **SAT**); 39 mg **CHOL**; 359 mg **SODIUM**; 51 g **CARB**; 4 g **FIBER**; 6 g **PRO**

Saturday Cinnamon Rolls

Even on busy weekends, you might fine time to bake these jump-start cinnamon rolls. Just thaw a couple loaves of frozen white bread dough or sweet roll dough the night before, and allow time for rising.

MAKES 16 servings   **PREP** 30 minutes   **RISE** 1 hour   **BAKE** 25 minutes at 375°F

½	**cup packed brown sugar**
1	**tablespoon ground cinnamon**
2	**16-ounce loaves frozen white bread dough or sweet roll dough, thawed**
3	**tablespoons butter, melted**
¾	**cup raisins (optional)**
1	**recipe Creamy Icing**

1 Grease two 9-inch round baking pans; set aside. In a small bowl stir together brown sugar and cinnamon; set aside.

2 On a lightly floured surface, roll each loaf of dough into a 12×8-inch rectangle, stopping occasionally to let dough relax if necessary. Brush with melted butter; sprinkle with brown sugar mixture. If desired, sprinkle with raisins.

3 Roll up from a short side, into a rectangle. Pinch dough to seal seams. Slice each rolled rectangle into eight equal pieces. Arrange in the prepared baking pans. Cover and let rise in a warm place until nearly double in size (about 1 hour).

4 Preheat oven to 375°F. Break any surface bubbles in rolls with a greased toothpick. Bake for 25 to 30 minutes or until rolls are golden and sound hollow when lightly tapped. If necessary to prevent overbrowning, cover rolls with foil the last 10 minutes of baking. Cool in pans on wire racks. Spread rolls with Creamy Icing. Serve warm.

Creamy Icing In a small bowl stir together 1½ cups powdered sugar, 1 tablespoon softened butter, and ½ teaspoon vanilla. Stir in 1 to 2 tablespoons whipping cream or milk, 1 teaspoon at a time, to make an icing of spreading consistency.

PER SERVING 242 **CAL**; 5 g **FAT** (2 g **SAT**); 8 mg **CHOL**; 290 mg **SODIUM**; 45 g **CARB**; 1 g **FIBER**; 3 g **PRO**

Apple-Streusel Muffins

Use a baking apple such as Granny Smith, McIntosh, or Golden Delicious in these moist autumnal muffins.

MAKES 12 servings   **PREP** 25 minutes   **BAKE** 18 minutes at 375°F   **COOL** 5 minutes

	Nonstick cooking spray
1	cup all-purpose flour
1	cup whole wheat flour or white whole wheat flour
⅓	cup packed brown sugar
2½	teaspoons baking powder
1	teaspoon apple pie spice
¼	teaspoon salt
2	eggs, lightly beaten
1	cup buttermilk
2	tablespoons canola oil
¾	cup shredded peeled apple (1 medium)
2	tablespoons finely chopped pecans
1	tablespoon flax seed meal or toasted wheat germ
1	tablespoon packed brown sugar
1	tablespoon butter

1 Preheat oven to 375°F. Lightly coat twelve 2½-inch muffin cups with cooking spray or line with paper bake cups and coat bake cups with cooking spray; set aside. In a large bowl stir together all-purpose flour, whole wheat flour, ⅓ cup brown sugar, baking powder, apple pie spice, and salt. Make a well in the center of flour mixture; set aside.

2 In a medium bowl combine eggs, buttermilk, and oil. Add egg mixture all at once to flour mixture. Stir just until moistened (batter should be lumpy). Fold in shredded apple. Spoon batter into the prepared muffin cups, filling each about three-fourths full.

3 For streusel topping, in a small bowl combine pecans, flax seed meal, and 1 tablespoon brown sugar. Using a pastry blender cut in butter until mixture resembles coarse crumbs. Spoon topping onto batter in cups.

4 Bake for 18 to 20 minutes or until a wooden toothpick inserted in centers comes out clean. Cool in muffin cups on a wire rack for 5 minutes. Remove muffins from muffin cups. Serve warm.

PER SERVING 163 **CAL**; 6 g **FAT** (1 g **SAT**); 39 mg **CHOL**; 167 mg **SODIUM**; 25 g **CARB**; 2 g **FIBER**; 4 g **PRO**

Zucchini-Chocolate Chip Scones

Shredded zucchini in these lower-fat scones give them tender texture, even with the smaller than typical amount of butter. Whole wheat flour adds fiber, while mini chocolate chips infuse each bite.

MAKES 6 servings   **PREP** 25 minutes   **BAKE** 13 minutes at 400°F

¾	**cup all-purpose flour**
½	**cup whole wheat flour**
1½	**tablespoons sugar**
¾	**teaspoon baking powder**
¼	**teaspoon ground cinnamon**
⅛	**teaspoon ground nutmeg**
⅛	**teaspoon baking soda**
⅛	**teaspoon salt**
2	**tablespoons butter, cut up**
¼	**cup refrigerated or frozen egg product, thawed, or 1 egg, lightly beaten**
¼	**cup buttermilk***
½	**cup shredded zucchini**
¼	**cup miniature semisweet chocolate pieces**

1 Preheat oven to 400°F. In a large bowl stir together all-purpose flour, whole wheat flour, sugar, baking powder, cinnamon, nutmeg, baking soda, and salt. Using a pastry blender, cut in butter until mixture resembles coarse crumbs. Make a well in center of the flour mixture.

2 In small bowl combine egg and buttermilk; stir in zucchini and chocolate pieces. Add the buttermilk mixture all at once to the flour mixture. Using a fork, stir just until moistened.

3 Turn dough out onto a lightly floured surface. Knead dough by folding and gently pressing it for 10 to 12 strokes or until nearly smooth. Pat or lightly roll dough into a 6-inch circle. Cut dough circle into six wedges.

4 Place wedges 2 inches apart on an ungreased baking sheet. Bake for 13 to 15 minutes or until edges are light brown. Remove scones from baking sheet; serve warm.

*Tip For a buttermilk substitute, place ¾ teaspoon lemon juice or vinegar in a glass measuring cup. Add enough fat-free milk to equal ¼ cup total liquid; stir. Let the mixture stand for 5 minutes before using it in the recipe.

PER SERVING 195 **CAL**; 7 g **FAT** (4 g **SAT**); 11 mg **CHOL**; 201 mg **SODIUM**; 29 g **CARB**; 2 g **FIBER**; 5 g **PRO**

Fruit Muesli

Muesli is a bit like untoasted granola. In parts of Europe, the mixture is often combined with milk or yogurt and refrigerated overnight for softer eating texture the next morning.

MAKES 12 servings   **START TO FINISH** 10 minutes

- **4 cups multigrain cereal with rolled rye, oats, barley, and wheat**
- **1 cup regular oats**
- **¾ cup coarsely chopped almonds or pecans, toasted***
- **1 cup toasted wheat germ**
- **1 7-ounce package mixed dried fruit bits**
- **½ cup unsalted sunflower kernels**
- **½ cup dried banana chips, coarsely crushed**
  Milk or fat-free plain yogurt (optional)

1 In a large bowl stir together multigrain cereal, oats, nuts, wheat germ, dried fruit bits, sunflower kernels, and banana chips.

2 Store muesli in an airtight container in the refrigerator up to 4 weeks. If desired, serve with milk or yogurt.

***Tip** To toast whole nuts or large pieces, spread them in a shallow pan. Bake at 350°F for 5 to 10 minutes, shaking the pan once or twice. Toast coconut in the same way, watching closely to avoid burning. Toast finely chopped or ground nuts or sesame seeds in a dry skillet over medium heat. Stir often to prevent burning.

PER SERVING 293 **CAL**; 10 g **FAT** (2 g **SAT**); 0 mg **CHOL**; 13 mg **SODIUM**; 44 g **CARB**; 4 g **FIBER**; 10 g **PRO**

CHAPTER 3

meals in minutes

To the table in just 30 minutes from the start, these dinners satisfy in no time.

CAJUN-RUBBED SALMON

Potato-Topped Beef Bowl

Here's quick comfort. These shepherd's pie-like bowls of goodness call on frozen mixed vegetables and instant mashed potato flakes for super quick prep time.

MAKES 4 servings   **START TO FINISH** 20 minutes

1   **pound lean ground beef**
1   **16-ounce package frozen mixed vegetables**
2   **cups shredded cheddar cheese (8 ounces)**
¼   **cup snipped fresh flat-leaf parsley**
¼   **teaspoon salt**
⅛   **teaspoon black pepper**
2   **cups boiling water**
2   **cups instant mashed potato flakes**
2   **tablespoons butter, melted**
     Salt
     Black pepper

1 Preheat broiler. In an extra-large skillet cook ground beef over medium-high heat until browned, using a wooden spoon to break up meat as it cooks. Drain off fat. Stir in frozen vegetables. Cook until heated through, stirring occasionally. Stir in 1 cup of the cheese, 2 tablespoons of the parsley, the ¼ teaspoon salt, and the ⅛ teaspoon pepper.

2 Meanwhile, in a large bowl combine the boiling water, potato flakes, and 1 tablespoon of the butter. Stir until smooth. Season with additional salt; set aside.

3 Divide meat and vegetable mixture among four 16-ounce broiler-safe dishes. Top with potatoes; sprinkle with the remaining 1 cup cheese. Broil 3 inches from heat for 2 to 3 minutes or until cheese is melted. Drizzle with remaining butter; sprinkle with remaining parsley. Sprinkle with pepper.

PER SERVING 677 **CAL**; 42 g **FAT** (22 g **SAT**); 152 mg **CHOL**; 692 mg **SODIUM**; 35 g **CARB**; 5 g **FIBER**; 41 g **PRO**

Tamale Pies

When you use individual-size dishes—which heat faster than one large dish—it's possible to put a bubbling casserole on the table in just 30 minutes from the time you walk in the door.

MAKES 4 servings   **PREP** 15 minutes   **BAKE** 15 minutes at 425°F

- 1   **pound lean ground beef**
- 1   **pound tomatoes, chopped**
- ½   **cup pitted olives (green, ripe, Kalamata, and/or Niçoise), coarsely chopped**
- ¼   **cup water**
- ½   **teaspoon salt**
- ½   **teaspoon black pepper**
- 1   **8.5-ounce package corn muffin mix**
- ½   **cup shredded cheddar cheese (2 ounces)**
  Coarsely chopped tomatoes and/or pitted olives (optional)
  Fresh cilantro leaves (optional)

1 Preheat oven to 425°F. In an extra-large skillet cook ground beef over medium-high heat until browned, using a wooden spoon to break up meat as it cooks. Drain off fat. Add the 1 pound tomatoes, the ½ cup olives, the water, salt, and pepper. Cook until heated through, stirring occasionally.

2 For topping, prepare corn muffin mix according to package directions. Divide hot meat mixture among four 12- to 16-ounce individual casseroles. Spoon topping over meat mixture; sprinkle with cheese.

3 Bake for 15 to 17 minutes or until a wooden toothpick inserted in topping comes out clean. If desired, garnish with additional tomatoes and/or olives and cilantro.

PER SERVING 609 **CAL**; 31 g **FAT** (11 g **SAT**); 147 mg **CHOL**; 1,052 mg **SODIUM**; 49 g **CARB**; 2 g **FIBER**; 32 g **PRO**

Spiced Pork Chops with Zucchini and Onions

Mild ground chile powder, brown sugar, salt, cocoa powder, and cayenne combine to create a flavorful glaze on these juicy grilled pork chops.

MAKES 4 servings   **PREP** 20 minutes   **GRILL** 11 minutes

1	tablespoon ground New Mexico chile pepper or chili powder
1½	teaspoons salt
1	teaspoon packed brown sugar
1	teaspoon unsweetened cocoa powder
¼	teaspoon cayenne pepper
4	bone-in pork loin chops, about 1 inch thick
6	to 7 small zucchini, cut lengthwise into ¼-inch-thick slices
1	tablespoon olive oil
1	teaspoon dried Mexican oregano or dried regular oregano, crushed
¼	teaspoon black pepper
½	cup crumbled queso fresco (2 ounces)
¼	cup snipped fresh cilantro
¼	cup finely chopped red onion
	Lime wedges

1 In a small bowl combine the ground chile pepper, 1 teaspoon of the salt, the brown sugar, cocoa powder, and cayenne pepper. Sprinkle evenly over all sides of the chops; rub in with your fingers.

2 Toss zucchini with oil to lightly coat. Season with the remaining ½ teaspoon salt, the dried oregano, and black pepper.

3 For a gas or charcoal grill, place chops on a greased grill rack directly over medium heat. Cover and grill for 11 to 13 minutes (150°F), turning once halfway through grilling time. Add the zucchini for the last 4 minutes of grilling; grill until crisp-tender, turning once.

4 Arrange zucchini and chops on serving plates. Top with queso fresco, cilantro, and red onion. Serve with lime wedges.

PER SERVING 385 **CAL**; 21 g **FAT** (5 g **SAT**); 95 mg **CHOL**; 1,005 mg **SODIUM**; 11 g **CARB**; 3 g **FIBER**; 37 g **PRO**

Pan-Seared Pork Burgers with Peppers and Mushrooms

For the lightest, most tender texture in the burgers, use a gentle touch when mixing and forming the patties. Packing the meat mixture too tightly creates dense, tough burgers.

MAKES 4 servings   **START TO FINISH** 25 minutes

2	medium red, yellow, and/or green sweet peppers
1	banana, jalapeño, or other chile pepper*, seeded and chopped (optional)
1	pound ground pork
3	teaspoons Worcestershire or soy sauce
2	teaspoons cracked black pepper
8	ounces sliced fresh mushrooms
	Salt
½	cup mayonnaise
	Black pepper
4	multigrain or plain hamburger buns, toasted if desired
	Sliced pickled jalapeño peppers (optional)
	Chips (optional)

1 Slice 1 sweet pepper into rings; set aside. Chop the remaining sweet pepper. In a large bowl combine chopped sweet peppers, chile pepper (if desired), the pork, 2 teaspoons of the Worcestershire sauce, and the 2 teaspoons cracked black pepper. Shape pork mixture into four ¾-inch-thick patties.

2 In a large hot skillet cook patties over medium-high for 10 to 12 minutes or until done (160°F), turning once halfway through cooking. Remove patties from skillet; keep warm. Add pepper rings and mushrooms to the hot skillet; cook for 3 minutes. Sprinkle with salt.

3 For sauce, combine mayonnaise and the remaining Worcestershire sauce. Season to taste with black pepper.

4 Place patties on bun bottoms; top with pepper-mushroom mixture. Spread cut sides of bun tops with sauce; place on patties. If desired, serve with pickled jalapeños and chips. Pass remaining sauce.

*Tip Because chile peppers contain volatile oils that can burn skin and eyes, avoid direct contact with them as much as possible. When working with chile peppers, wear plastic or rubber gloves. If bare hands do touch the peppers, wash hands and nails well with soap and warm water.

PER SERVING 629 **CAL**; 47 g **FAT** (13 g **SAT**); 92 mg **CHOL**; 593 mg **SODIUM**; 26 g **CARB**; 4 g **FIBER**; 26 g **PRO**

Sweet Potato, Sausage, and Green Pepper Hash

This colorful, nutrient-packed and egg-topped hash makes a nice brunch dish or casual supper.

MAKES 4 servings   **START TO FINISH** 35 minutes

- **2** small sweet potatoes, peeled, halved lengthwise, and cut in ½-inch slices (about 10 ounces)
- **12** ounces bulk pork sausage
- **1** fresh Anaheim pepper (see tip, page 54) or green sweet pepper, seeded and chopped
- **4** cups spinach and/or baby kale
- **½** teaspoon ground cumin
- **½** medium orange
- **1** tablespoon olive oil
- **4** eggs
- **⅛** teaspoon salt
- **⅛** teaspoon crushed red pepper

1 In an extra-large skillet bring 2 tablespoons water to boiling over medium heat. Add sweet potatoes; cover and cook for 12 minutes.

2 Uncover skillet, add sausage and chile pepper. Cook over medium-high heat until sausage is browned and sweet potatoes are tender, stirring occasionally to break up sausage. Drain off fat, if necessary. Stir in spinach and cumin; squeeze orange half over spinach; cook and stir 1 to 2 minutes or until wilted. Transfer hash to a serving dish; cover to keep warm.

3 Add oil to skillet. Heat over medium heat. Crack eggs into skillet; sprinkle with salt and crushed red pepper. Cover skillet. Cook for 2 to 3 minutes or until desired doneness. Serve over hash.

PER SERVING 474 **CAL**; 35 g **FAT** (12 g **SAT**); 251 mg **CHOL**; 830 mg **SODIUM**; 19 g **CARB**; 3 g **FIBER**; 21 g **PRO**

Mexican Skillet Dinner

Topping this homey skillet with shredded lettuce and chopped fresh tomato right before serving makes it a truly one-dish meal—just one pot is used to cook and serve the whole thing.

MAKES 6 servings **START TO FINISH** 25 minutes

12   **ounces uncooked Mexican chorizo or pork sausage, casings removed if present**
2   **cups frozen whole kernel corn**
1   **14.5-ounce can diced tomatoes, undrained**
1   **cup uncooked instant rice**
½   **cup water**
2   **teaspoons chili powder**
½   **teaspoon ground cumin**
1   **15-ounce can pinto beans, rinsed and drained**
¾   **cup shredded Mexican cheese blend or Colby and Monterey Jack cheese (3 ounces)**
  Shredded lettuce (optional)
  Chopped fresh tomato (optional)

1 In a large skillet cook chorizo over medium heat until no longer pink, using a wooden spoon to break up meat as it cooks. Using a slotted spoon, remove chorizo and drain on paper towels. Drain off fat from skillet.

2 In the same skillet combine corn, canned tomatoes, rice, the water, chili powder, and cumin. Bring to boiling; reduce heat. Simmer, covered, for 5 minutes or until liquid is absorbed and rice is tender. Stir in beans and cooked chorizo; heat through. Remove from heat.

3 Sprinkle with cheese. Cover; let stand for 2 to 3 minutes or until cheese is slightly melted. If desired, top with lettuce and fresh tomato.

PER SERVING 230 **CAL**; 27 g **FAT** (11 g **SAT**); 13 mg **CHOL**; 585 mg **SODIUM**; 38 g **CARB**; 5 g **FIBER**; 23 g **PRO**

Creamy Alfredo with Bacon and Peas

It doesn't take much whipping cream—just ¼ to ⅓ cup—to give this pasta dish luxurious taste and texture. With bacon, Parmesan cheese, and sweet peas, it will appeal to even the pickiest eaters.

MAKES 4 servings   **START TO FINISH** 35 minutes

4	slices thick-sliced bacon, coarsely chopped
2	cloves garlic, minced
8	ounces dried rotini, penne, or rigatoni pasta
1	14.5-ounce can chicken broth
1	cup water
½	teaspoon salt
¼	teaspoon freshly ground black pepper
1	cup frozen peas
¼	to ⅓ cup whipping cream
¼	cup grated Parmesan cheese
	Crumbled, crisp-cooked bacon (optional)

1 In a large deep skillet cook the 4 slices chopped bacon over medium heat until crisp. Add garlic; cook and stir for 30 seconds more. Drain off fat. Stir in pasta, broth, the water, salt, and pepper.

2 Bring to boiling; reduce heat. Simmer, covered, for 12 to 15 minutes or until pasta is tender but still firm, stirring once. Stir in peas, whipping cream, and cheese. Cook and stir about 2 minutes more or until heated through. If desired, sprinkle with crumbled bacon.

PER SERVING 378 **CAL**; 13 g **FAT** (6 g **SAT**); 37 mg **CHOL**; 1,043 mg **SODIUM**; 49 g **CARB**; 3 g **FIBER**; 16 g **PRO**

Basque Chicken

Made on the stovetop, this dish takes 30 minutes. You can also stir it together in the morning and let it simmer in your slow cooker all day—either 10 hours on low or 5 hours on high.

MAKES 6 servings   **START TO FINISH** 30 minutes

- 1¼ **pounds skinless, boneless chicken thighs, cut into 2-inch pieces**
- ½ **teaspoon salt**
- ¼ **teaspoon black pepper**
- 1 **tablespoon olive oil**
- 1 **onion, thinly sliced**
- 1 **red sweet pepper, cut into ¼-inch strips**
- 2 **cloves garlic, minced**
- 1 **14.5-ounce can diced tomatoes, drained**
- 12 **ounces small red potatoes, cut into ½-inch wedges**
- 1 **cup chicken broth**
- 1 **teaspoon fresh snipped thyme or ¼ teaspoon dried thyme, crushed**
- ½ **teaspoon dried savory, crushed**
- ⅓ **cup small pimiento-stuffed olives**
  Fresh thyme (optional)

1 Sprinkle chicken with ¼ teaspoon of the salt and black pepper. In a large Dutch oven heat oil over medium-high heat. Add chicken; cook for 4 minutes or until lightly browned, turning once halfway through cooking.

2 Add onion and sweet pepper to Dutch oven; cook for 3 minutes or until crisp-tender. Add garlic; cook 30 seconds more. Add tomatoes, potatoes, broth, the 1 teaspoon fresh thyme or ¼ teaspoon dried thyme, the savory, and remaining ¼ teaspoon salt. Bring to boiling; reduce heat. Simmer, covered, for 20 minutes or until chicken and potatoes are tender. Remove from heat. Stir in olives. If desired, garnish with additional fresh thyme.

Slow Cooker Directions In a 3½- or 4-quart slow cooker combine chicken, potatoes, sweet pepper, and onion. Stir in tomatoes, broth, garlic, savory, the 1 teaspoon thyme, ¼ teaspoon salt, and the black pepper. Cover and cook on low-heat setting for 10 to 11 hours or on high-heat setting for 5 to 5½ hours. Stir in olives and, if desired, garnish with additional fresh thyme.

PER SERVING 204 **CAL**; 6 g **FAT** (1 g **SAT**); 79 mg **CHOL**; 576 mg **SODIUM**; 16 g **CARB**; 3 g **FIBER**; 21 g **PRO**

Crispy Lemon Chicken with Shortcut Risotto

Arborio rice has a high starch content that contributes to the creamy, toothsome texture of risotto. Arborio rice is called for here—the stoveside stirring of the traditional risotto method is not.

MAKES 4 servings   **START TO FINISH** 30 minutes

- 2   **14.5-ounce cans reduced-sodium chicken broth**
- 1⅓ **cups arborio rice or short grain white rice**
- ½   **cup chopped onion (1 medium)**
- 2   **teaspoons finely shredded lemon peel**
- 2   **tablespoons lemon juice**
- 4   **6-ounce skinless, boneless chicken breast halves**
- ¾   **cup panko bread crumbs**
- ⅓   **cup grated Parmesan cheese**
- 1   **teaspoon dried oregano, crushed**
- 2   **eggs, lightly beaten**
- ¼   **cup milk**
- 3   **tablespoons olive oil or vegetable oil**
- 1½ **cups frozen peas**
- ½   **cup grated Parmesan cheese**
-        **Julienned lemon peel (optional)**
-        **Fresh flat-leaf parsley leaves (optional)**

1 In a medium saucepan combine broth, rice, onion, and lemon juice. Bring mixture to boiling; reduce heat. Cover and simmer for 18 minutes.

2 Meanwhile, place each chicken breast half between two pieces of plastic wrap. Using the flat side of a meat mallet, pound chicken lightly to about ¼-inch thickness. Discard plastic wrap.

3 In a shallow dish stir together bread crumbs, ⅓ cup Parmesan cheese, oregano, and the lemon peel. In a second dish stir together eggs and milk. Dip chicken into egg mixture then into crumb mixture to coat.

4 In an extra-large skillet heat oil over medium heat. Add chicken (half at a time, if needed); cook for 2 to 3 minutes on each side or until golden and chicken is no longer pink (170°F). Transfer chicken to a cutting board.

5 Stir peas into the risotto. Cover and cook for 3 minutes more (do not lift lid). Stir in the ½ cup grated Parmesan cheese. To serve, slice chicken. Place risotto on a serving dish and top with sliced chicken. If desired, top with julienned lemon peel and parsley.

PER SERVING 704 **CAL**; 22 g **FAT** (6 g **SAT**); 218 mg **CHOL**; 1,063 mg **SODIUM**; 66 g **CARB**; 4 g **FIBER**; 57 g **PRO**

Chicken Curry Skillet with Rice Noodles

Just a small amount of prepared Thai red curry paste gives this Asian-style dish a powerful flavor punch. Add the larger amount if you like your food to have more heat.

MAKES 6 servings   **START TO FINISH** 30 minutes

8	ounces dried wide rice noodles, broken
2	tablespoons vegetable oil
1½	pounds skinless, boneless chicken breast halves, cut into strips
1	16-ounce package frozen desired stir-fry vegetables, thawed
1	14-ounce can unsweetened light coconut milk
½	cup water
1	tablespoon sugar
1	tablespoon fish sauce
½	to 1 teaspoon red curry paste
¼	teaspoon salt
¼	teaspoon black pepper
¼	cup snipped fresh basil

1 Soak rice noodles according to package directions; drain.

2 In an extra-large skillet heat oil over medium-high heat. Add chicken; cook and stir for 8 to 10 minutes or until chicken is no longer pink, adding stir-fry vegetables for the last 4 minutes of cooking. Remove chicken mixture from skillet.

3 In the same skillet combine coconut milk, the water, sugar, fish sauce, curry paste, salt, and pepper. Bring to boiling. Stir in rice noodles and chicken mixture. Return to boiling; reduce heat. Simmer, uncovered, about 2 minutes or until noodles are tender but still firm and sauce is thickened. Sprinkle with basil.

PER SERVING 386 **CAL**; 10 g **FAT** (3 g **SAT**); 66 mg **CHOL**; 529 mg **SODIUM**; 42 g **CARB**; 2 g **FIBER**; 28 g **PRO**

MEDITERRANEAN
PIZZA SKILLET

Mediterranean Pizza Skillet

This skillet meal is a bit like a deconstructed pizza—chicken, tomatoes, artichokes, feta cheese, crusty bread, and lots of fresh greens.

MAKES 4 servings   **START TO FINISH** 30 minutes

- 2   **tablespoons olive oil**
- 1   **pound skinless, boneless chicken breast halves, cut into ¾-inch pieces**
- 2   **cloves garlic, minced**
- 1   **14-ounce can quartered artichoke hearts, drained**
- 1⅓ **cups chopped roma tomatoes (4 medium)**
- 1   **2.25-ounce can sliced pitted ripe olives, drained**
- ½   **teaspoon dried Italian seasoning, crushed**
- ¼   **teaspoon ground black pepper**
- 2   **cups romaine lettuce or mesclun mix, chopped**
- 1   **cup crumbled feta cheese (4 ounces)**
- ⅓   **cup fresh basil leaves, shredded or torn**
      Crusty Italian or French bread slices, toasted

1 In a large skillet heat oil over medium-high heat. Add chicken and garlic; cook and stir for 2 to 4 minutes or until chicken is browned. Stir in artichoke hearts, tomatoes, olives, Italian seasoning, and pepper.

2 Bring to boiling; reduce heat. Simmer, covered, for 10 minutes or until chicken is no longer pink. Top with lettuce and cheese. Cook, covered, for 1 to 2 minutes more or just until lettuce begins to wilt. Sprinkle with basil. Serve on or with toasted bread slices.

PER SERVING 395 **CAL**; 17 g **FAT** (6 g **SAT**); 82 mg **CHOL**; 1,003 mg **SODIUM**; 27 g **CARB**; 6 g **FIBER**; 33 g **PRO**

Chicken-Peanut Sauce Stir-Fry

Customize this peanut-sauced chicken dish with the stir-fry vegetable blend of your choice.

MAKES 4 servings   **START TO FINISH** 25 minutes

- 1   **14-ounce can unsweetened light coconut milk**
- ⅓   **cup peanut butter**
- ½   **teaspoon salt**
- ½   **teaspoon ground ginger**
- ¼   **teaspoon crushed red pepper**
- 1   **pound skinless, boneless chicken breast halves, cut into 1-inch pieces**
      Salt
      Black pepper
- 1   **tablespoon canola oil or vegetable oil**
- 2   **cups frozen stir-fry vegetables**
- ½   **cup frozen peas**
- 4   **cups hot cooked ramen noodles or rice**

1 For sauce, in a medium bowl whisk together coconut milk, peanut butter, the ½ teaspoon salt, the ginger, and crushed red pepper. Set aside.

2 Sprinkle chicken lightly with additional salt and black pepper. In a large skillet or wok heat oil over medium-high heat. Add chicken; cook about 6 minutes or until no longer pink, turning to brown evenly. Remove from skillet.

3 Add stir-fry vegetables and peas to hot skillet. Cook and stir for 2 to 3 minutes or until heated through.

4 Add sauce to skillet; return chicken. Gently stir all ingredients together to coat with sauce; heat through. Serve stir-fry over ramen noodles.

PER SERVING 754 **CAL**; 37 g **FAT** (15 g **SAT**); 73 mg **CHOL**; 836 mg **SODIUM**; 64 g **CARB**; 5 g **FIBER**; 42 g **PRO**

One-Pan Chicken Flatbreads

Nearly seedless English cucumbers are longer and more slender than regular slicing cucumbers. Look for them wrapped in plastic in the produce section of your supermarket.

MAKES 4 servings **START TO FINISH** 35 minutes

½	**cup roasted garlic hummus**
½	**cup plain Greek yogurt**
12	**ounces skinless, boneless chicken breast halves**
4	**teaspoons lemon-pepper seasoning**
1	**tablespoon olive oil**
4	**7-inch flatbread rounds**
½	**cup halved grape tomatoes**
½	**cup sliced English cucumber**
¼	**cup chopped onion**
¼	**cup crumbled feta cheese (1 ounce)**
	Snipped fresh flat-leaf parsley (optional)
	Plain Greek yogurt (optional)
	Lemon wedges (optional)

1 In a small bowl combine hummus and the ½ cup yogurt; set aside. Place each chicken breast half between two pieces of plastic wrap. Using the flat side of a meat mallet, pound chicken lightly to about ¼-inch thickness. Remove plastic wrap. Sprinkle chicken with lemon-pepper seasoning.

2 In an extra-large skillet heat oil over medium-high heat. Add chicken in batches; cook for 4 to 6 minutes or until chicken is no longer pink, turning once. Transfer to a cutting board; let stand for 2 minutes. Cut chicken into strips. Carefully wipe skillet dry.

3 Add flatbreads to the same skillet. Cook over medium-high heat for 2 to 4 minutes or until toasted, turning once.

4 Top flatbreads with chicken, tomatoes, cucumber, onion, and cheese. If desired, sprinkle with parsley. Serve with hummus and, if desired, additional yogurt and lemon wedges.

PER SERVING 517 **CAL**; 23 g **FAT** (6 g **SAT**); 66 mg **CHOL**; 925 mg **SODIUM**; 45 g **CARB**; 5 g **FIBER**; 32 g **PRO**

Turkey Burgers and Home Fries

Curried mayonnaise adds flavor and moistness to super-lean turkey breast burgers—which can be dry when overcooked. The flavored mayo also gets spread on the pita flatbreads before serving.

MAKES 4 servings   **START TO FINISH** 30 minutes

½   **cup mayonnaise**
2   **teaspoons curry powder**
2   **tablespoons olive oil**
2   **cups refrigerated sliced potatoes**
    Salt and black pepper
½   **cup crumbled basil-and-tomato-flavor feta cheese (2 ounces)**
¼   **teaspoon salt**
1   **pound ground turkey breast**
4   **Greek pita flatbreads**
    Red onion slices (optional)
    Fresh spinach (optional)
    Crumbled basil-and-tomato-flavor feta cheese (optional)

1 Preheat broiler. For the spread, in a small bowl combine mayonnaise and curry powder; set aside. In an extra-large skillet heat oil over medium-high heat. Add potatoes; sprinkle with salt and pepper. Cook for 6 minutes. Turn potatoes; cook about 6 minutes more or until crisp.

2 Meanwhile, in a medium bowl combine 2 tablespoons of the spread, the ½ cup cheese, and the ¼ teaspoon salt. Add ground turkey; mix well. Shape meat into four ½-inch-thick patties.

3 Place patties on the unheated rack of a broiler pan.* Broil about 4 inches from the heat for 11 to 13 minutes or until no longer pink (165°F), turning once.

4 Spread flatbreads with the remaining spread. Add red onion, the patties, spinach, and, if desired, additional cheese; fold in half. Serve with potatoes.

* For a gas or charcoal grill, place patties on the grill rack directly over medium heat. Cover and grill for 10 minutes or until done (160°F), turning once halfway through grilling.

PER SERVING 658 **CAL**; 33 g **FAT** (6 g **SAT**); 91 mg **CHOL**; 1,033 mg **SODIUM**; 51 g **CARB**; 3 g **FIBER**; 38 g **PRO**

Cajun-Rubbed Salmon

A little bit of brown sugar in the Cajun rub creates a nice spicy crust on the salmon during cooking. See photo, page 48.

MAKES 4 servings   **START TO FINISH** 30 minutes

- 4   **6-ounce fresh or frozen boneless salmon fillets**
- ½   **cup slivered red onion**
- ½   **cup chopped celery (1 stalk)**
- 2   **tablespoons snipped fresh flat-leaf parsley**
- 2   **tablespoons chopped dill pickle**
- 1   **tablespoon dill pickle juice**
- 1   **tablespoon olive oil**
- 2   **teaspoons Dijon mustard**
- ¼   **teaspoon salt**
   Dash sugar
- 2   **tablespoons Cajun Seasoning or purchased Cajun seasoning**
- 2   **tablespoons olive oil**

1 Thaw salmon, if frozen. Preheat oven to 400°F. For relish, in a small bowl combine onion, celery, parsley, pickle, pickle juice, the 1 tablespoon oil, the mustard, salt, and sugar. Cover and chill until ready to serve (up to 1 hour).

2 Rinse salmon; pat dry with paper towels. Measure thickness of salmon. Sprinkle salmon with Cajun Seasoning; rub in with your fingers.

3 In a large cast-iron or other heavy oven-going skillet heat the 2 tablespoons oil over medium-high heat. Add salmon, skin side up; cook for 2 to 3 minutes or until lightly browned. Turn salmon. Place skillet in oven. Roast until salmon begins to flake when tested with a fork. (Allow 4 to 6 minutes per ½-inch thickness of salmon, including browning time.)

4 Stir relish. Serve salmon with relish.

Cajun Seasoning In a small bowl combine 2 tablespoons packed brown sugar; 2 tablespoons paprika; 1 tablespoon kosher salt; 2 teaspoons dried oregano, crushed; 2 teaspoons dried thyme, crushed; 1 teaspoon garlic powder; 1 teaspoon ground cumin; ½ teaspoon crushed red pepper; and ¼ teaspoon cayenne pepper. Store in an airtight container.

PER SERVING 356 **CAL**; 21 g **FAT** (3 g **SAT**); 94 mg **CHOL**; 778 mg **SODIUM**; 5 g **CARB**; 1 g **FIBER**; 34 g **PRO**

Skillet Bucatini with Spring Vegetables

Bucatini are thick strands of hollow-tube pasta. If you can't find it, use thick or regular spaghetti instead.

MAKES 4 servings   **START TO FINISH** 35 minutes

- 4   **ounces dried bucatini**
- 2   **tablespoons peanut oil or vegetable oil**
- 12   **ounces asparagus spears, trimmed and cut into 2-inch pieces (2½ cups)**
- 6   **cloves garlic, sliced**
- 3   **cups red and yellow cherry tomatoes, halved**
- ¾   **teaspoon salt**
- ¾   **cup snipped fresh basil**
- ½   **cup halved pitted Kalamata olives**
- ¼   **teaspoon freshly ground black pepper**
- ½   **cup grated Parmesan cheese**
   Lemon wedges (optional)

1 In a large Dutch oven cook pasta according to package directions. Drain, reserving ½ cup of the cooking water. Return pasta to hot pan. Drizzle with 1 tablespoon of the oil; toss gently to coat.

2 Heat an extra-large skillet over high heat. Add the remaining 1 tablespoon oil.

3 Add asparagus; cook and stir for 2 minutes or until bright green. Add garlic; cook and stir for 10 seconds or until fragrant. Add cherry tomatoes and ½ teaspoon of the salt; cook and stir for 30 seconds. Add basil and olives; cook and stir 30 seconds more. Remove from heat.

4 Gently stir in cooked pasta, the remaining ¼ teaspoon salt, and pepper. Stir in enough of the reserved pasta cooking water to reach desired consistency. Sprinkle with cheese and, if desired, serve with lemon wedges.

PER SERVING 278 **CAL**; 13 g **FAT** (3 g **SAT**); 9 mg **CHOL**; 785 mg **SODIUM**; 33 g **CARB**; 5 g **FIBER**; 11 g **PRO**

SKILLET BUCATINI
WITH SPRING
VEGETABLES

Skillet Vegetables on Cheese Toast

Thick slices of toasty whole grain bread are spread with goat cheese, then broiled and topped with fresh, lightly caramelized baby carrots, red onion, and mushrooms.

MAKES 4 servings   **START TO FINISH** 25 minutes

2	tablespoons olive oil
8	fresh button mushrooms, halved
½	8-ounce package peeled fresh baby carrots, halved lengthwise
1	small red onion, cut into thin wedges
4	cloves garlic, coarsely chopped
2	tablespoons water
	Salt
	Black pepper
8	slices hearty whole grain bread
4	ounces soft goat cheese (chèvre)
	Olive oil (optional)
	Fresh basil (optional)

1 Preheat broiler. In a large skillet heat the 2 tablespoons oil over medium-high heat. Add mushrooms, carrots, onion, and garlic; cook and stir for 2 to 3 minutes or just until vegetables begin to brown. Add the water; reduce heat to medium. Cook, covered, about 5 minutes or until vegetables are crisp-tender, stirring once. Sprinkle with salt and pepper.

2 Meanwhile, for cheese toast, place bread slices on a baking sheet. Broil about 3 inches from the heat for 1 to 2 minutes or until lightly toasted. Spread with goat cheese. Broil for 1 to 2 minutes more or until cheese is softened.

3 To serve, spoon vegetables on cheese toast. If desired, drizzle with additional oil and sprinkle with basil.

PER SERVING 461 **CAL**; 21 g **FAT** (6 g **SAT**); 13 mg **CHOL**; 596 mg **SODIUM**; 56 g **CARB**; 8 g **FIBER**; 15 g **PRO**

Falafel Patty Melt

Turn a can of garbanzo beans into quick falafel with the help of a food processor.

MAKES 4 servings   **START TO FINISH** 25 minutes

½	cup frozen peas
1	15-ounce can garbanzo beans (chickpeas), rinsed and drained
½	cup shredded carrot (1 medium)
2	tablespoons all-purpose flour
2	tablespoons olive oil
½	teaspoon black pepper
¼	teaspoon salt
4	flatbreads or pita bread rounds
8	slices dilled Havarti cheese, shredded (4 to 6 ounces)
	Romaine lettuce leaves (optional)
	chopped tomato (optional)

1 Preheat oven to 400°F. Place peas in a 1-quart microwave-safe dish; cover with vented plastic wrap. Microwave on high for 2 minutes. Set aside.

2 In a food processor combine garbanzo beans, carrot, flour, 1 tablespoon of the oil, the pepper, and salt. Cover and process with on/off pulses until nearly smooth. Transfer mixture to a large bowl. (Or combine ingredients in a large bowl; use an immersion blender to puree.) Stir in peas. Shape mixture into eight patties.

3 In a large nonstick skillet heat the remaining 1 tablespoon oil over medium-high heat. Add patties. Cook for 4 to 6 minutes or until browned and heated through, turning once.

4 Meanwhile, place flatbreads on a baking sheet; top with cheese. Bake for 5 minutes or until cheese is melted. Place two patties on each warm flatbread. Fold flatbread over patties. If desired, serve with lettuce and tomato.

PER SERVING 508 **CAL**; 17 g **FAT** (7 g **SAT**); 21 mg **CHOL**; 1,006 mg **SODIUM**; 66 g **CARB**; 8 g **FIBER**; 18 g **PRO**

FALAFEL PATTY MELT

cook it slowly

Plan ready-when-you-are slow cooker meals for any day of the week.

CLASSIC BEEF STROGANOFF

BEEF

Classic Beef Stroganoff, 75

Flank Steak Hoagies with
Roasted Red Pepper Sauce, 72

Moroccan-Style Short Ribs, 74

Pot Roast with Fruit and Chipotle Sauce, 72

PORK

Italian Wild Rice Soup, 79

Loaded Bratwurst Stew, 78

Pasta with Arrabbiata Sauce, 80

Sassy Pork Chops, 77

CHICKEN AND TURKEY

Chicken Enchilada Casserole, 84

Greek Breast of Turkey, 87

Orange Chicken with Olives, 81

Pesto Chicken Sandwich, 82

Post-Thanksgiving Pot Pie, 87

Sweet Potato and Pepper Jack Grits with Chicken, 85

Pot Roast with Fruit and Chipotle Sauce

This sweet and spicy twist on traditional pot roast combines smoky chipotle peppers with a melange of dried fruits. Serve it with hot buttered noodles and steamed green beans.

MAKES 8 servings **PREP** 15 minutes
SLOW COOK 10 hours (low) or 5 hours (high)

- 1   **3-pound boneless beef chuck pot roast**
- 2   **teaspoons garlic pepper seasoning**
- 1   **7-ounce package mixed dried fruit**
- ½   **cup water**
- 1   **tablespoon finely chopped chipotle peppers in adobo sauce**
- 1   **tablespoon cold water**
- 2   **teaspoons cornstarch**
     Fresh cilantro sprigs (optional)

1 Trim fat from meat. If necessary, cut meat to fit into a 3½- or 4-quart slow cooker. Sprinkle both sides of meat with garlic pepper seasoning. Place meat in cooker. Add dried fruit, ½ cup water, and chipotle peppers.

2 Cover and cook on low-heat setting for 10 to 11 hours or on high-heat setting for 5 to 5½ hours. Transfer meat and fruit to a serving platter; cover with foil to keep warm.

3 For sauce, pour cooking liquid into a bowl or glass measuring cup. Skim off fat. In a medium saucepan combine 1 tablespoon cold water and cornstarch; stir in cooking liquid. Cook and stir over medium heat until thickened and bubbly. Cook and stir for 2 minutes more.

4 Thinly slice meat. Serve meat and fruit with sauce. If desired, sprinkle with cilantro.

PER SERVING 275 **CAL**; 6 g **FAT** (2 g **SAT**); 101 mg **CHOL**; 378 mg **SODIUM**; 17 g **CARB**; 1 g **FIBER**; 37 g **PRO**

Flank Steak Hoagies with Roasted Red Pepper Sauce

Smoked paprika is magic dust for food. Just a small amount imparts wonderfully warm, smoky flavor. Sold in both sweet and hot varieties, the hot variety is labeled as such.

MAKES 6 servings **PREP** 25 minutes
SLOW COOK 7 hours (low) or 3½ hours (high)

- 1   **12-ounce jar roasted red sweet peppers, drained**
- ¼   **cup chopped green onions (2)**
- ¼   **cup reduced-sodium chicken broth, dry white wine, or water**
- 1   **tablespoon balsamic vinegar or sherry vinegar**
- 1½   **teaspoons snipped fresh thyme or ½ teaspoon dried thyme, crushed**
- 2   **cloves garlic, minced**
- ¼   **to ½ teaspoon smoked paprika or dash cayenne pepper**
- ¼   **teaspoon salt**
- 1½   **pounds beef flank steak**
     Salt and black pepper
- 6   **hoagie buns, split and toasted**
- ¾   **cup crumbled soft goat cheese (chèvre) (3 ounces)**
- 1   **cup firmly packed fresh basil leaves**
- ½   **small red onion, thinly sliced**

1 For sauce, in a food processor or blender combine roasted peppers, green onions, broth, vinegar, thyme, garlic, paprika, and ¼ teaspoon salt. Cover and process or blend until nearly smooth. Set aside.

2 Trim fat from meat. Sprinkle both sides of meat with additional salt and black pepper. If necessary, cut meat to fit into a 3½- or 4-quart slow cooker. Add meat to cooker. Pour sauce over meat.

3 Cover and cook on low-heat setting for 7 to 8 hours or on high-heat setting for 3½ to 4 hours. Transfer meat to a cutting board, reserving sauce. Thinly slice meat diagonally across the grain or shred meat using two forks.

4 Spread bottom bun with cheese. Arrange meat in buns. If desired, spoon sauce over meat. Top with basil and red onion.

PER SERVING 494 **CAL**; 15 g **FAT** (6 g **SAT**); 80 mg **CHOL**; 747 mg **SODIUM**; 55 g **CARB**; 3 g **FIBER**; 34 g **PRO**

FLANK STEAK HOAGIES WITH
ROASTED RED PEPPER SAUCE

Moroccan-Style Short Ribs

Almonds, olives, and garbanzo beans—and spices such as ginger and cinnamon—give these short ribs North African flavor. They're served over fluffy couscous—another Moroccan staple.

MAKES 8 servings   **PREP** 30 minutes   **SLOW COOK** 9 hours (low) or 4½ hours (high)

- 3½ **pounds beef short ribs**
- 1 **tablespoon dried thyme, crushed**
- 1 **teaspoon salt**
- 1 **teaspoon ground ginger**
- 1 **teaspoon black pepper**
- ½ **teaspoon ground cinnamon**
- 2 **tablespoons olive oil**
- 3 **cups beef broth**
- 1 **15-ounce can garbanzo beans (chickpeas), rinsed and drained**
- 1 **14.5-ounce can diced tomatoes, undrained**
- 1 **large onion, cut into thin wedges**
- 1 **medium fennel bulb, trimmed and cut into thin wedges**
- 1 **cup chopped carrots (2 medium)**
- 4 **cloves garlic, minced**
- 1 **10-ounce package couscous**
- ½ **cup sliced almonds, toasted (see tip, page 47)**
- ½ **cup pitted kalamata olives, halved**

1 Trim fat from short ribs. For rub, in a small bowl combine thyme, salt, ginger, pepper, and cinnamon. Sprinkle rub evenly over ribs; rub in with your fingers. In a large skillet cook ribs, half at a time, in hot oil over medium-high heat until browned on all sides. Drain off fat. In a 6- to 7-quart slow cooker combine broth, beans, tomatoes, onion, fennel, carrots, and garlic. Top with ribs.

2 Cover and cook on low-heat setting for 9 to 10 hours or on high-heat setting for 4½ to 5 hours.

3 Before serving, prepare couscous according to package directions. Stir in almonds and olives.

4 Using a slotted spoon, transfer short ribs and vegetables to a serving dish. If desired, spoon some of the cooking liquid over ribs and vegetables. Serve with couscous.

PER SERVING 441 **CAL**; 17 g **FAT** (4 g **SAT**); 46 mg **CHOL**; 1,064 mg **SODIUM**; 45 g **CARB**; 6 g **FIBER**; 26 g **PRO**

Classic Beef Stroganoff

In the 1950s this Russian dish of tender chunks of beef and mushrooms in a rich sour cream sauce was considered the height of elegance. The slow cooker makes a special dinner possible any day of the week.

MAKES 6 servings   **PREP** 30 minutes   **SLOW COOK** 8 hours (low) or 4 hours (high) + 30 minutes (high)

1½	**pounds beef stew meat**
1	**tablespoon vegetable oil**
2	**cups sliced fresh mushrooms**
½	**cup chopped onion (1 medium)**
2	**cloves garlic, minced**
½	**teaspoon dried oregano, crushed**
½	**teaspoon salt**
¼	**teaspoon dried thyme, crushed**
¼	**teaspoon black pepper**
1	**bay leaf**
1½	**cups reduced-sodium beef broth**
⅓	**cup dry sherry**
1	**8-ounce carton light sour cream**
¼	**cup cold water**
2	**tablespoons cornstarch**
	Hot cooked egg noodles (optional)
	Chopped green onions (optional)

1 Trim fat from meat. Cut meat into 1-inch pieces. In a large skillet heat oil over medium heat. Cook meat, half at a time, in hot oil until browned. Drain off fat. Set aside.

2 In a 3½- or 4-quart slow cooker combine mushrooms, onion, garlic, oregano, salt, thyme, pepper, and bay leaf. Top with meat. Pour broth and sherry over all.

3 Cover and cook on low-heat setting for 8 to 10 hours or on high-heat setting for 4 to 5 hours.

4 Remove bay leaf. If using low-heat setting, turn to high-heat setting. In a medium bowl combine sour cream, the cold water, and cornstarch. Stir about 1 cup of the hot cooking liquid into sour cream mixture. Stir sour cream mixture into cooker. Cover and cook about 30 minutes more or until thickened. If desired, serve stroganoff over cooked egg noodles and sprinkle each serving with chopped green onions.

PER SERVING 248 **CAL**; 9 g **FAT** (4 g **SAT**); 79 mg **CHOL**; 408 mg **SODIUM**; 8 g **CARB**; 1 g **FIBER**; 28 g **PRO**

Sassy Pork Chops

The classic Cajun trio of sweet peppers, celery, and onion plus spicy Mexican chipotle peppers give this dish attitude—in the tastiest way.

MAKES 8 servings   **PREP** 25 minutes   **SLOW COOK** 6 hours (low) or 3 hours (high)

2   cups red, green, and/or yellow sweet pepper strips (2 medium)
1   cup thinly sliced celery (2 stalks)
½   cup chopped onion (1 medium)
8   pork loin chops, cut ¾ inch thick
½   teaspoon garlic salt
¼   teaspoon black pepper
2   tablespoons vegetable oil
¼   cup reduced-sodium chicken broth
¼   cup orange juice
1   tablespoon chopped canned chipotle peppers in adobo sauce
½   teaspoon dried oregano, crushed
    Hot cooked rice (optional)

1 In a 4- to 5-quart slow cooker combine sweet peppers, celery, and onion; set aside. Trim fat from chops. Sprinkle chops with garlic salt and black pepper. In an extra-large skillet cook chops, half at a time, in hot oil over medium-high heat until browned on both sides. Transfer chops to cooker. In a small bowl combine broth, orange juice, chipotle peppers, and oregano. Pour over chops in cooker.

2 Cover and cook on low-heat setting for 6 to 7 hours or on high-heat setting for 3 to 3½ hours.

3 Discard cooking liquid. If desired, serve chops and vegetables over hot cooked rice.

PER SERVING 215 **CAL**; 7 g **FAT** (1 g **SAT**); 78 mg **CHOL**; 363 mg **SODIUM**; 4 g **CARB**; 1 g **FIBER**; 33 g **PRO**

Loaded Bratwurst Stew

Cut a few fat grams from this German-style stew by using turkey bratwurst, if you like.

MAKES 6 servings   **PREP** 20 minutes   **SLOW COOK** 6 hours (low) or 3 hours (high)

4	cups coarsely chopped green cabbage
1	pound cooked smoked bratwurst, cut into ½-inch slices
1½	cups coarsely chopped red-skin potatoes
¾	cup chopped red sweet pepper (1 medium)
1	medium onion, cut into thin wedges
2	14.5-ounce cans chicken broth
1	tablespoon spicy brown mustard
1	tablespoon cider vinegar
¼	teaspoon salt
¼	teaspoon black pepper
⅛	teaspoon celery seeds
	Shredded Swiss cheese (optional)

1 In a 5- to 6-quart slow cooker combine cabbage, bratwurst, potatoes, sweet pepper, and onion. In a large bowl stir together broth, mustard, vinegar, salt, black pepper, and celery seeds. Pour over mixture in cooker.

2 Cover and cook on low-heat setting for 6 to 7 hours or on high-heat setting for 3 to 3½ hours. If desired, top each serving with cheese.

PER SERVING 315 **CAL**; 23 g **FAT** (8 g **SAT**); 49 mg **CHOL**; 1,348 mg **SODIUM**; 15 g **CARB**; 3 g **FIBER**; 12 g **PRO**

Italian Wild Rice Soup

Adding freshness to a slow-cooked soup or stew is as simple as stirring in a fresh ingredient right before serving, as with the spinach here. Just a minute or two in the hot soup wilts it yet it retains its bright green color.

MAKES 8 servings   **PREP** 25 minutes   **SLOW COOK** 7 hours (low) or 3½ hours (high)

1	pound ground pork
4	cups water
2	14.5-ounce cans lower-sodium beef broth
1	14.5-ounce can no-salt-added diced tomatoes with basil, garlic, and oregano, undrained
1	6-ounce can tomato paste
1	cup chopped onion (1 large)
¾	cup wild rice, rinsed and drained
6	cloves garlic, minced
2	tablespoons Italian seasoning, crushed
1½	teaspoons paprika
1	teaspoon fennel seeds
½	teaspoon black pepper
¼	teaspoon salt
¼	teaspoon crushed red pepper
1	9-ounce package fresh spinach, chopped
½	cup finely shredded Parmesan cheese (2 ounces)

1 In a large skillet cook pork over medium heat until no longer pink, using a wooden spoon to break up meat as it cooks; drain off fat.

2 In a 4- to 6-quart slow cooker combine cooked pork, the water, broth, tomatoes, tomato paste, onion, uncooked wild rice, garlic, Italian seasoning, paprika, fennel seeds, black pepper, salt, and crushed red pepper.

3 Cover and cook on low-heat setting for 7 to 8 hours or on high-heat setting for 3½ to 4 hours. Stir spinach into soup.

4 Top individual servings with cheese.

PER SERVING 274 **CAL**; 11 g **FAT** (5 g **SAT**); 45 mg **CHOL**; 315 mg **SODIUM**; 24 g **CARB**; 6 g **FIBER**; 20 g **PRO**

Pasta with Arrabbiata Sauce

"Arrabbiata" means "angry" in Italian. It refers to the heat contributed by crushed red pepper in this classic sauce. It's not overly spicy but it does have zing! Orecchiette or "little ears" are perfect shapes to capture the chunky sauce.

MAKES 8 servings   **PREP** 20 minutes   **SLOW COOK** 8 hours (low) or 4 hours (high)

1	large onion, cut into thin wedges
5	ounces pancetta, chopped, or 5 slices bacon, chopped
3	cloves garlic, minced
4	14.5-ounce cans diced tomatoes with basil, garlic, and oregano, undrained
1	15-ounce can tomato sauce
2	teaspoons dried parsley
1	teaspoon dried oregano, crushed
½	teaspoon salt
½	teaspoon dried basil, crushed
½	teaspoon crushed red pepper
8	cups hot cooked orecchiette or penne pasta
¼	cup shaved or finely shredded Parmesan cheese (1 ounce)
	Fresh oregano leaves (optional)

1 In a large skillet cook onion, pancetta, and garlic over medium heat until onion is tender and pancetta is browned. Drain off fat.

2 Transfer onion mixture to a 3½- to 5-quart slow cooker. Stir in tomatoes, tomato sauce, parsley, dried oregano, salt, basil, and crushed red pepper.

3 Cover and cook on low-heat setting for 8 to 10 hours or on high-heat setting for 4 to 5 hours.

4 Serve sauce over cooked pasta. Sprinkle each serving with cheese and, if desired, garnish with fresh oregano.

PER SERVING 369 **CAL**; 8 g **FAT** (3 g **SAT**); 14 mg **CHOL**; 1,131 mg **SODIUM**; 59 g **CARB**; 5 g **FIBER**; 13 g **PRO**

Orange Chicken with Olives

The sweetness of dried apricots and orange juice pairs nicely with briny, salty olives. Serve this saucy chicken over pearl (also called Israeli) couscous or rice.

MAKES 12 servings   **PREP** 20 minutes   **SLOW COOK** 5 hours (low) or 2½ hours (high)

4	cloves garlic, slivered
⅓	cup all-purpose flour
¼	teaspoon salt
¼	teaspoon black pepper
12	chicken drumsticks and/or thighs, skinned
1	cup dried apricots
1	cup whole pimiento-stuffed green olives
1	bay leaf
1	cup orange juice
¼	cup balsamic vinegar
2	tablespoons honey
1	teaspoon dried thyme, crushed
1	teaspoon finely shredded orange peel
	Snipped fresh flat-leaf parsley
	Hot cooked couscous or rice

1 Sprinkle garlic in a 5- to 6-quart slow cooker; set aside. In a large resealable plastic bag combine flour, salt, and pepper. Add chicken pieces, a few at a time; seal bag and shake to coat. Place chicken on garlic in slow cooker. Sprinkle with remaining flour mixture. Top with apricots, olives, and bay leaf.

2 In a small bowl stir together orange juice, vinegar, honey, thyme, and orange peel. Add to slow cooker.

3 Cover and cook on low-heat setting for 5 to 5½ hours or on high-heat setting for 2½ to 3 hours. Discard bay leaf. Sprinkle with snipped fresh parsley. Serve with hot cooked couscous or rice.

PER SERVING 203 **CAL**; 5 g **FAT** (1 g **SAT**); 79 mg **CHOL**; 306 mg **SODIUM**; 16 g **CARB**; 1 g **FIBER**; 22 g **PRO**

Pesto Chicken Sandwich

Sweet pepper and summer squash are added to the slow cooker just 30 minutes before serving to keep them fresh, bright in color, and crisp-tender.

MAKES 6 servings   **PREP** 30 minutes   **SLOW COOK** 4 hours (low) or 2 hours (high) + 30 minutes (high)

1	teaspoon dried Italian seasoning, crushed
¼	teaspoon salt
¼	teaspoon black pepper
1	pound skinless, boneless chicken breast halves
3	cups sliced fresh mushrooms (8 ounces)
1	large onion, thinly sliced
2	cloves garlic, minced
1	14.5-ounce can diced tomatoes, undrained
2	tablespoons red wine vinegar
1½	cups green, red, and/or yellow sweet pepper strips (1 large)
1	medium yellow summer squash or zucchini, halved lengthwise and sliced ¼ inch thick (1¼ cups)
⅓	cup mayonnaise or salad dressing
2	tablespoons basil pesto
1	8 x 12-inch focaccia, cut in half horizontally
½	cup shredded provolone cheese (2 ounces)

1 For the rub, in a small bowl combine Italian seasoning, salt, and black pepper. Sprinkle rub evenly over both sides of chicken; rub in with your fingers.

2 In a 3½- or 4-quart slow cooker combine chicken, mushrooms, onion, and garlic. Pour tomatoes and vinegar over chicken in cooker.

3 Cover and cook on low-heat setting for 4 to 5 hours or on high-heat setting for 2 to 2½ hours.

4 If using low-heat setting, turn to high-heat setting. Add sweet pepper and squash. Cover and cook 30 minutes more.

5 Meanwhile, in a small bowl combine mayonnaise and pesto. Spread evenly over cut sides of focaccia. Transfer chicken to a cutting board; thinly slice chicken. Arrange chicken slices on bottom half of focaccia. Using a slotted spoon, spoon vegetable mixture over chicken. Sprinkle with cheese. Replace top half of focaccia. Cut into wedges.

PER SERVING 439 **CAL**; 18 g **FAT** (4 g **SAT**); 63 mg **CHOL**; 770 mg **SODIUM**; 43 g **CARB**; 3 g **FIBER**; 29 g **PRO**

Chicken Enchilada Casserole

This is the quick and easy way to make enchiladas. Tortillas are torn and layered with other ingredients instead of being stuffed and rolled. Same great taste but a whole lot easier!

MAKES 8 servings   **PREP** 15 minutes   **SLOW COOK** 5 hours (low) or 2½ hours (high)   **STAND** 15 minutes

    Nonstick cooking spray
9 6-inch corn tortillas
1 11-ounce can whole kernel corn with sweet peppers, drained
1 6-ounce package refrigerated cooked Southwestern-flavor chicken breast strips, chopped
1 4-ounce can diced green chile peppers, undrained
2 cups shredded Mexican-style four cheese blend (8 ounces)
1 19-ounce can enchilada sauce
1 15-ounce can black beans, rinsed and drained
1 7-ounce package refrigerated avocado dip (guacamole)
½ cup sour cream
    Chopped tomato (optional)
    Snipped fresh cilantro (optional)

1 Lightly coat the inside of a 3½- or 4-quart slow cooker with cooking spray. Tear three of the tortillas and place in the prepared cooker, overlapping as necessary. Top with corn, half the chicken, and half the chile peppers; sprinkle with ½ cup of the cheese. Pour about ¾ cup of the enchilada sauce over layers in cooker.

2 Repeat with three more tortillas, the black beans, the remaining chicken, and the remaining chile peppers; sprinkle with another ½ cup of the cheese. Pour another ¾ cup of the enchilada sauce over mixture. Top with the remaining three torn tortillas, the remaining 1 cup cheese, and the remaining enchilada sauce.

3 Cover and cook on low-heat setting for 5 hours or on high-heat setting for 2½ hours. Turn off cooker. If possible, remove crockery liner from cooker. Let stand, covered, for 15 minutes before serving. Serve with avocado dip and sour cream. If desired, sprinkle with chopped tomato and fresh cilantro.

PER SERVING 348 **CAL**; 17 g **FAT** (7 g **SAT**); 45 mg **CHOL**; 1,141 mg **SODIUM**; 34 g **CARB**; 6 g **FIBER**; 18 g **PRO**

Sweet Potato and Pepper Jack Grits with Chicken

Be sure to use regular grits in this recipe. Most of what you find on the supermarket shelves is either quick-cooking (5 minutes) or instant. Regular hominy grits are often labeled "old-fashioned"—similar to oats.

MAKES 6 servings   **PREP** 15 minutes   **SLOW COOK** 7 hours (low) or 3½ hours (high)   **STAND** 5 minutes

- **1** pound skinless, boneless chicken thighs, cut into 1-inch pieces
- **3** cups water
- **1** 15- to 15.5-ounce can mashed sweet potatoes or cut sweet potatoes*
- **1** 12-ounce can (1½ cups) evaporated milk
- **1** cup regular (hominy) grits
- **½** teaspoon salt
- **½** teaspoon black pepper
- **2** tablespoons butter, cut up
- **1½** cups shredded Monterey Jack cheese with jalapeño peppers (6 ounces)
- **¼** cup snipped fresh cilantro

1 Line a 3½- or 4-quart slow cooker with disposable slow cooker liner. In prepared cooker combine chicken, the water, sweet potatoes, evaporated milk, grits, salt, and pepper.

2 Cover and cook on low-heat setting for 7 to 9 hours or on high-heat setting for 3½ to 4½ hours.

3 Turn off cooker. Cover and let stand for 5 minutes. Top each serving with some of the butter and cheese. Sprinkle with cilantro.

* If using cut sweet potatoes, drain and mash them before adding to the slow cooker.

PER SERVING 478 **CAL**; 21 g **FAT** (12 g **SAT**); 119 mg **CHOL**; 595 mg **SODIUM**; 45 g **CARB**; 3 g **FIBER**; 30 g **PRO**

GREEK BREAST OF TURKEY

Greek Breast of Turkey

If you can find Greek oregano, use it in this Mediterranean-inspired dish. It's more fragrant and flavorful than regular oregano.

MAKES 8 servings   **PREP** 30 minutes
SLOW COOK 5½ hours (low)

1	**4- to 5-pound boneless uncooked turkey breast**
1	**cup chopped onion (1 large)**
½	**cup pitted and halved Kalamata olives**
½	**cup oil-packed dried tomatoes, drained and cut into slivers**
½	**cup low-sodium chicken broth**
2	**teaspoons finely shredded lemon peel**
3	**tablespoons lemon juice**
2	**cloves garlic, minced**
½	**teaspoon salt**
½	**teaspoon dried oregano, crushed**
¼	**teaspoon dried rosemary, crushed**
¼	**teaspoon dried thyme, crushed**
¼	**teaspoon black pepper**
3	**tablespoons all-purpose flour**

1 Place turkey breast in a 4-quart slow cooker. Add onion, olives, dried tomatoes, ¼ cup of the broth, the lemon peel, lemon juice, garlic, salt, oregano, rosemary, thyme, and pepper.

2 Cover and cook on low-heat setting for 5½ to 6 hours. Transfer turkey breast to a serving platter, reserving cooking liquid. Cover turkey breast loosely with foil to keep warm.

3 For lemon sauce, in a medium saucepan whisk together flour and the remaining ¼ cup broth until smooth. Stir in cooking liquid. Bring to boiling over medium heat; reduce heat. Simmer, uncovered, for 8 to 10 minutes or until thickened, stirring frequently. Slice turkey and serve with lemon sauce.

PER SERVING 416 **CAL**; 19 g **FAT** (5 g **SAT**); 147 mg **CHOL**; 407 mg **SODIUM**; 8 g **CARB**; 2 g **FIBER**; 51 g **PRO**

Post-Thanksgiving Pot Pie

After cooking a Thanksgiving feast, this easy-on-the-cook dish offers a welcome way to serve leftovers. It's "pot pie" in reverse—the mixture of turkey, vegetables and gravy is served on top of warm biscuits or rolls.

MAKES 6 servings   **PREP** 15 minutes
SLOW COOK 4 hours (low) or 2 hours (high)

3	**cups chopped leftover cooked turkey**
1	**cup leftover cooked green beans or frozen cut green beans**
1	**cup leftover cooked corn or frozen whole kernel corn**
1	**cup frozen small whole onions**
1	**cup thinly sliced carrots (2 medium)**
½	**cup thinly sliced celery (1 stalk)**
½	**teaspoon dried thyme, crushed**
2	**cups leftover turkey gravy or purchased turkey gravy**
2	**tablespoons quick-cooking tapioca, crushed**
6	**leftover biscuits, dinner rolls, or croissants, warmed and split**

1 In a 3½- or 4-quart slow cooker combine turkey, green beans, corn, onions, carrots, celery, and thyme. In a small bowl combine gravy and tapioca. Pour gravy mixture over mixture in cooker; stir to combine.

2 Cover and cook on low-heat setting for 4 to 5 hours or on high-heat setting for 2 to 2½ hours.

3 To serve, place warm biscuits on dinner plates. Spoon turkey over biscuits.

PER SERVING 514 **CAL**; 25 g **FAT** (13 g **SAT**); 122 mg **CHOL**; 764 mg **SODIUM**; 45 g **CARB**; 3 g **FIBER**; 27 g **PRO**

CHAPTER 5

great grilling

Flame-kissed foods—from burgers to chops to lime-glazed shrimp on a stick.

GRILLED CHILE-LIME
SHRIMP

BEEF

Red-Eye Burgers, 90

Sarsaparilla-Glazed Wild West Burgers and
Southwest Sweet Potatoes, 93

Steak and Herb Tacos, 94

PORK

Cowboy Pork Burgers, 99

Dijon Pork Chops with Apple Salad, 97

Mustard-Rubbed Pork Loin with Rhubarb Sauce, 98

Spicy Hoisin-Honey Ribs, 94

CHICKEN

Chorizo-Chicken Burgers, 100

Golden Grilled Chicken Thighs with Apricots, 101

FISH AND SEAFOOD

Grilled Chile-Lime Shrimp, 105

Grilled Shrimp Panzanella, 103

Sesame-Ginger Tuna Steaks, 102

MEATLESS

Smoked Tomato Po' Boy Sandwiches, 105

Red-Eye Burgers

A dry rub of ground coffee, brown sugar, paprika, salt, pepper, and dried thyme is pressed onto the exterior of the patties before grilling to create a flavorful crust on the burgers.

MAKES 4 servings   **PREP** 30 minutes   **GRILL** 10 minutes

1	tablespoon ground coffee beans (not instant)
1½	teaspoons packed brown sugar
1½	teaspoons smoked paprika or regular paprika
1½	teaspoons black pepper
1	teaspoon kosher salt
½	teaspoon dried thyme, crushed
¼	cup ketchup
2	tablespoons prepared horseradish
1	tablespoon Worcestershire sauce
	Bottled hot pepper sauce
2	tablespoons vegetable oil
¾	cup thinly sliced shallots (6 medium)
	Salt and black pepper
1⅓	pounds 85% lean ground beef
4	pretzel or kaiser rolls, split and toasted
4	slices sharp cheddar cheese
8	large butterhead (Boston or bibb) lettuce leaves
½	cup dill pickle slices

1 For red-eye rub, in a small bowl stir together ground coffee, brown sugar, paprika, 1½ teaspoons black pepper, kosher salt, and thyme; set aside.

2 For horseradish-ketchup sauce, in a small bowl combine ketchup, horseradish, and Worcestershire sauce. Season to taste with hot pepper sauce; set aside.

3 In a small skillet heat oil over medium heat. Add shallots; cook for 3 to 4 minutes or until lightly browned and crisp, stirring frequently. Using a slotted spoon, remove shallots and drain on paper towels. Sprinkle with salt and additional black pepper.

4 Shape ground beef into four ½-inch-thick patties. Generously coat both sides of patties with red-eye rub, pressing into meat to adhere.

5 For a charcoal or gas grill, place patties on the grill rack directly over medium heat. Cover and grill for 10 to 13 minutes or until done (160°F), turning once halfway through grilling. Add rolls, cut sides down, to grill the last 2 minutes of grilling or until toasted on one side. Add cheese slices to patties the last 1 minute of grilling or until cheese is melted.

6 To serve, arrange lettuce and pickle slices on bottoms of rolls; add patties. Top with horseradish-ketchup sauce and fried shallots. Replace roll tops.

PER SERVING 689 **CAL**; 39 g **FAT** (14 g **SAT**); 122 mg **CHOL**; 1,514 mg **SODIUM**; 46 g **CARB**; 3 g **FIBER**; 40 g **PRO**

Sarsaparilla-Glazed Wild West Burgers and Southwest Sweet Potatoes

Garlic lovers gather each year to revel in the "stinking bulb" at the Gilroy Garlic Festival in Gilroy, California. In 2014, Suzanne Clark of Phoenix, Arizona, was one of them—and she took the top prize of $5,000 with her recipe for these hearty bison burgers. Suzanne describes herself as an "extreme planner"—and you kind of have to be to make them. The bit of effort it takes is worth every tasty bite.

MAKES 6 servings   **PREP** 1 hour 30 minutes   **BAKE** 40 minutes at 400°F   **GRILL** 10 minutes

12	slices thick cut peppered bacon
4	teaspoons butter
⅔	cup chopped shallots
4	cups Sarsaparilla soda or root beer (not diet)
2	tablespoons balsamic vinegar
1	tablespoon cornstarch
⅔	cup mayonnaise
6	cloves garlic, minced
1	chipotle pepper in adobo sauce, finely chopped
2	teaspoons finely shredded lime peel
1½	pounds ground bison
½	pound ground chorizo sausage
3	green onions, chopped
1	teaspoon salt
6	onion buns, split
1	recipe Wrangler Relish
1	recipe Southwest Sweet Potatoes

1 Preheat oven to 400°F. Place bacon on a rack fitted in a baking sheet. Bake for 20 minutes or until bacon is crisp. Set aside. For the Sarsaparilla Glaze, in a large cast-iron skillet add butter and shallots. Cook over medium heat for 2 to 3 minutes or until shallots soften. In a large bowl stir together the Sarsaparilla, vinegar, and cornstarch (mixture will foam). Add to skillet. Bring to boiling; reduce heat and cook, uncovered, for 30 minutes or until reduced to about 1 cup and glaze is thick and syrupy, stirring occasionally.

2 For the cowboy sauce, in a small bowl combine mayonnaise, 2 of the minced garlic cloves, chipotle, and lime peel. Cover and chill until needed.

3 For the patties, in a large bowl combine bison, chorizo, green onions, the remaining garlic, and salt. Divide into six portions and form 4-inch patties. For a charcoal or gas grill, brush grill rack with oil. Place patties on grill rack directly over medium heat. Cover and grill for 10 to 12 minutes or until done (160°F), turning once. Place patties in skillet with Sarsaparilla Glaze, turning to coat.

4 To assemble burgers, place 2 slices bacon followed by a patty on bottom portion of each bun. Drizzle with sauce in the pan. Top with Wrangler Relish. Generously spread cowboy sauce on cut side of bun top; place on patty. Serve with Southwest Sweet Potatoes.

Wrangler Relish In a saucepan combine ⅔ cup water, ⅔ cup vinegar, ¼ cup packed brown sugar, 1 tablespoon pickling spice wrapped in 100% cotton cheesecloth, and 1 teaspoon salt; bring to boiling. Add 1 cup chopped sweet onion and 14 cloves garlic, peeled and sliced. Simmer, uncovered, for 10 minutes. Remove from heat; add 1 cup peeled and chopped jicama. Let relish stand at least 30 minutes. Meanwhile, preheat oven to 400°F. Line a baking sheet with foil. Brush 1 tablespoon vegetable oil on 1 fresh poblano chile pepper, halved (see tip, page 54); ½ medium sweet red pepper; and 1 ear fresh sweet corn, husks and silks removed. Place on prepared baking sheet. Roast for 20 minutes or until lightly charred. Set corn aside until cool. Wrap peppers in the foil; let stand 20 minutes. Remove charred skin from peppers; chop peppers. Remove corn from the cob. Drain and discard liquid from relish; discard spice bag. Stir corn and peppers into relish.

Southwest Sweet Potatoes Preheat oven to 400°F. For the seasoning, in a small bowl combine 2 tablespoons sugar, 2½ teaspoons smoked paprika, 2 teaspoons ground ancho chile pepper, 2 teaspoons ground cinnamon, and 1 teaspoon sea salt. Line a baking pan with foil, add 3 cups sweet potatoes, peeled and diced; ½ cup chopped onion; and ½ cup chopped red sweet pepper. Sprinkle seasoning on vegetables then drizzle with 2 tablespoons vegetable oil; stir. Bake for 20 to 30 minutes or until vegetables are tender, stirring 5 cloves minced garlic into vegetables halfway through cooking. Transfer potatoes to a serving dish; top with ¼ cup snipped fresh flat-leaf parsley.

PER SERVING 1,483 **CAL**; 86 g **FAT** (25 g **SAT**); 196 mg **CHOL**; 3,591 mg **SODIUM**; 105 g **CARB**; 9 g **FIBER**; 72 g **PRO**

Steak and Herb Tacos

Serve these smoky tacos with refried beans, Mexican rice—and margaritas, if you like.

MAKES 6 servings   **PREP** 25 minutes
MARINATE 2 hours   **GRILL** 14 minutes

- 1   to 1½ pounds lean boneless beef top sirloin steak, 1 inch thick
- 2   tablespoons snipped fresh marjoram or oregano or 2 teaspoons dried marjoram or oregano, crushed
- 1   tablespoon chili powder
- 2   teaspoons garlic powder
- ¼   teaspoon salt
- ¼   teaspoon cayenne pepper
- 1   tablespoon olive oil or vegetable oil
- 12 6- to 8-inch corn or flour tortillas
- 2   tomatoes, chopped
- 1   small onion, chopped
- 4   to 6 radishes with tops, sliced
- ½   cup snipped fresh cilantro
- 8   to 10 ounces queso fresco cheese, crumbled or Monterey Jack cheese, shredded
      Lime wedges (optional)

1 Trim fat from steak. In a small bowl combine marjoram, chili powder, garlic powder, salt, cayenne pepper, and oil. Spread rub on both sides of steak. Place steak in a large resealable plastic bag set in a shallow bowl. Seal bag; turn to coat steak. Marinate in the refrigerator for 2 to 4 hours, turning the bag once or twice.

2 Drain steak, discarding marinade. For a charcoal or gas grill, place steaks on the grill rack directly over medium heat. Cover and grill for 14 to 18 minutes for medium rare (145°F) or 18 to 22 minutes for medium (160°F), turning once halfway through grilling. Meanwhile, wrap tortillas in foil. Place on grill during the last 10 minutes of grilling, turning occasionally.

3 Slice or coarsely chop steak. Serve in warm tortillas with tomatoes, onion, radishes, cilantro, and cheese. Pass lime wedges, if desired.

PER SERVING 189 CAL; 8 g FAT (2 g SAT); 18 mg CHOL; 115 mg SODIUM; 16 g CARB; 2 g FIBER; 14 g PRO

Spicy Hoisin-Honey Ribs

Although it's no longer considered necessary to soak wood chunks before smoking, the wood smokes more when wet. If you forgot to soak it, you will still get delicious results.

MAKES 4 servings   **PREP** 15 minutes
CHILL 1 hour   **SMOKE** 3 hours

- 1   tablespoon paprika
- ½   teaspoon coarsely ground black pepper
- ¼   teaspoon onion salt
- 4   pounds pork loin back ribs (2 racks)
- 1   lime, halved
- 6   to 8 oak or hickory wood chunks*
- 1   to 2 tablespoons finely chopped canned chipotle peppers in adobo sauce
- ½   cup bottled hoisin sauce
- ¼   cup honey
- 2   tablespoons cider vinegar
- 2   tablespoons Dijon mustard
- 2   cloves garlic, minced

1 For rub, in a small bowl stir together paprika, black pepper, and onion salt. Trim fat from ribs. Place ribs in a shallow dish. Squeeze lime halves over ribs and rub the cut surfaces of the lime halves over ribs. Sprinkle the rub evenly over ribs; rub in with your fingers. Cover and chill for 1 to 4 hours.

2 In a smoker arrange preheated coals, wood chunks, and water pan according to the manufacturer's directions. Pour water into pan. Place ribs, bone sides down, on the grill rack over water pan. (Or place ribs in a rib rack; place on grill rack over pan.) Cover and smoke for 3 to 4 hours or until tender. Add additional coals and water as needed to maintain temperature and moisture.

3 Meanwhile, for sauce, in a small saucepan stir together the chipotle peppers, hoisin sauce, honey, vinegar, mustard, and garlic. Cook and stir over low heat until heated through. Before serving, brush ribs with some of the sauce. Pass remaining sauce.

*Note: For the most smoke production, soak wood chunks in enough water to cover for at least 1 hour before grilling. Drain wood chips before using.

PER SERVING 509 CAL; 25 g FAT (8 g SAT); 110 mg CHOL; 898 mg SODIUM; 40 g CARB; 1 g FIBER; 28 g PRO

SPICY HOISIN-HONEY RIBS

Dijon Pork Chops with Apple Salad

The ingredients for the salad can be tossed together and the blue cheese vinaigrette can be made and refrigerated several hours ahead of serving time.

MAKES 4 servings   **PREP** 30 minutes   **GRILL** 10 minutes   **STAND** 5 minutes

3	cups baby arugula or watercress
1	Fuji apple, cored, quartered, and thinly sliced
1	cup thinly sliced celery (2 stalks)
½	cup thinly sliced radishes
½	cup pecan pieces, toasted (see tip, page 47)
3	tablespoons cider vinegar
3	tablespoons olive oil
1	tablespoon honey
¼	cup crumbled blue cheese (1 ounce)
	Kosher salt or salt
	Black pepper
2	tablespoons Dijon mustard
1	tablespoon whole grain mustard
1	tablespoon mayonnaise or salad dressing
2	teaspoons packed brown sugar
2	teaspoons snipped fresh thyme or ½ teaspoon dried thyme, crushed
¼	teaspoon black pepper
4	bone-in pork loin chops, about 1 inch thick

1 For salad, in a large bowl toss together arugula, apple, celery, radishes, and pecans; cover and chill. For dressing, in a small bowl whisk together vinegar, oil, honey, and blue cheese. Season with salt and pepper; cover and chill.

2 For the mustard sauce, in a small bowl whisk together Dijon mustard, whole grain mustard, mayonnaise, brown sugar, thyme, and the ¼ teaspoon pepper; set aside.

3 For a charcoal or gas grill, place chops on the grill rack directly over medium heat. Cover and grill for 10 to 12 minutes or until 145°F, turning once halfway through grilling. Transfer chops to a plate and let stand for 5 minutes. Spoon mustard sauce over chops.

4 Toss salad with dressing; serve with chops.

PER SERVING 542 **CAL**; 38 g **FAT** (8 g **SAT**); 105 mg **CHOL**; 627 mg **SODIUM**; 17 g **CARB**; 3 g **FIBER**; 33 g **PRO**

Mustard-Rubbed Pork Loin with Rhubarb Sauce

The natural sweetness of pork is particularly well suited to pairing with fruits such as apples, pears, peaches—and rhubarb. Although botanically a vegetable, tart rhubarb is almost always sweetened and prepared like fruit.

MAKES 8 servings   **PREP** 30 minutes   **GRILL** 45 minutes

- 1   **2- to 2½-pound boneless pork top loin roast (single loin)**
- ¼   **cup Dijon mustard**
- 1   **tablespoon snipped fresh rosemary**
- 6   **to 12 cloves garlic, minced**
- ½   **teaspoon salt**
- ¼   **teaspoon black pepper**
- 3   **cups sliced rhubarb (about 1 pound)**
- ⅓   **cup orange juice**
- 1   **tablespoon cider vinegar**
- ⅓   **to ½ cup sugar**

1 Trim fat from meat. Score top and bottom of meat in a diamond pattern by making shallow diagonal cuts at 1-inch intervals. For rub, in a small bowl combine mustard, rosemary, garlic, salt, and pepper. Spread over all sides of meat; rub in with your fingers.

2 For a charcoal grill, arrange medium coals around a drip pan. Test for medium-low heat above pan. Place meat on grill rack over drip pan. Cover and grill for 45 minutes to 1 hour or until an instant-read thermometer inserted in center of meat registers 145°F. (For a gas grill, preheat grill. Reduce heat to medium-low. Adjust for indirect cooking. Grill as above, except place meat on a rack in a roasting pan; place pan on grill rack.) Remove meat from grill. Cover with foil; let stand while preparing Rhubarb Sauce.

3 For Rhubarb Sauce, in a medium saucepan stir rhubarb, orange juice, vinegar, and sugar. Bring to boiling; reduce heat. Cover and simmer about 15 minutes or until rhubarb is tender.

4 To serve, slice roast and serve with warm Rhubarb Sauce.

PER SERVING 175 **CAL**; 4 g **FAT** (1 g **SAT**); 60 mg **CHOL**; 358 mg **SODIUM**; 12 g **CARB**; 1 g **FIBER**; 22 g **PRO**

Cowboy Pork Burgers

If there were a way to improve on bacon, this recipe offers it up. The bacon for these indulgent burgers is "country fried"—dipped in buttermilk and coated in seasoned flour before frying.

MAKES 6 servings   **PREP** 15 minutes   **CHILL** 30 minutes   **GRILL** 8 minutes

¾	cup barbecue sauce
1	to 2 fresh jalapeños, seeded and finely chopped (see tip, page 54)
1	tablespoon barbecue seasoning
1½	pounds ground pork
1	recipe Country Fried Bacon
1	large sweet onion
1	tablespoon balsamic vinegar
	Olive oil
	Kosher salt
6	English muffins, split and toasted
6	slices sharp cheddar or Monterey Jack cheese with jalapeño peppers
	Black pepper
	Pickle slices (optional)

1 In a medium bowl combine ¼ cup of the barbecue sauce, the jalapeños, and barbecue seasoning. Add ground pork; mix gently until combined. Shape meat into six patties slightly larger than the English muffins. Cover and chill for at least 30 minutes.

2 Cut onion into ½-inch slices. Brush with vinegar and oil, keeping rings intact.

3 Brush both sides of pork patties with oil; sprinkle lightly with salt.

4 For a charcoal or gas grill, place pork patties and onion slices on the grill rack directly over medium heat. Cover and grill for 8 to 10 minutes or until patties are done (160°F) and onion slices are tender and slightly charred, turning once halfway through grilling. Add English muffins, cut sides down, to grill rack the last 2 minutes of grilling or until toasted. Add cheese slices to patties for the last 1 minute of grilling or until cheese is melted.

5 Place onion slices in a bowl; toss to separate into rings. Sprinkle with salt and black pepper. To serve, spread the remaining ½ cup barbecue sauce on cut sides of English muffin halves. Add burgers, Country Fried Bacon, grilled onions, and English muffin tops. If desired, thread wooden skewers with pickle slices; insert skewers into sandwiches.

Country Fried Bacon In a shallow dish combine ½ cup all-purpose flour, 1½ teaspoons black pepper, ½ teaspoon kosher salt, and ½ teaspoon garlic powder. In a second shallow dish combine ½ cup buttermilk and 2 tablespoons milk. Cut 6 slices of bacon in half crosswise; separate slices. Working with one piece at a time, coat bacon in flour mixture, shaking off excess. Coat with buttermilk mixture; coat in flour mixture again, adding additional flour, if needed. Line a baking sheet with paper towels. In a Dutch oven heat 1½ inches peanut or vegetable oil over medium heat to 350°F. Fry bacon in batches for 4 minutes or until golden and crisp, turning once halfway through cooking. Drain on paper towels. Serve warm.

PER SERVING 730 **CAL**; 42 g **FAT** (15 g **SAT**); 113 mg **CHOL**; 1,358 mg **SODIUM**; 55 g **CARB**; 3 g **FIBER**; 35 g **PRO**

Chorizo-Chicken Burgers

Poblano peppers are the glossy dark green peppers used in chiles rellenos, the classic Mexican dish of deep-fried, cheese-stuffed chiles. They are generally mild and fruity with just a hint of heat.

MAKES 6 servings   **PREP** 30 minutes   **CHILL** 30 minutes   **GRILL** 34 minutes   **STAND** 15 minutes

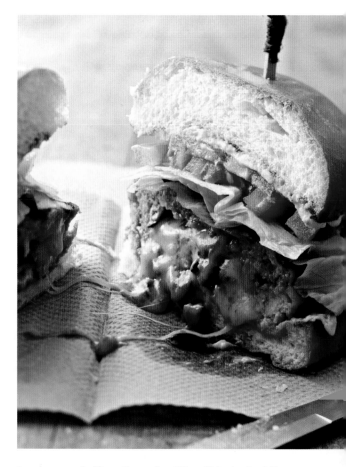

8	ounces cooked chorizo sausage, casings removed and thinly sliced
2	cloves garlic
½	cup chopped onion (1 medium)
1½	pounds uncooked ground chicken or turkey
2	teaspoons ground ancho chile pepper
¾	teaspoon kosher salt
1	medium avocado, halved, seeded, and peeled
⅓	cup mayonnaise
2	fresh poblano chile peppers (see tip, page 54)
½	cup shredded Monterey Jack cheese with jalapeño peppers (2 ounces)
6	hamburger buns, split and, if desired, toasted Iceberg lettuce leaves, sliced tomato, and/or sliced onion (optional)

1 In a food processor combine sausage and garlic. Pulse until sausage is finely chopped. Add ½ cup chopped onion; pulse until onion is finely chopped. Transfer sausage mixture to a large bowl. Add ground chicken, ground ancho pepper, and salt; mix gently until combined. Shape meat into twelve ¼-inch-thick patties. Cover and chill at least 30 minutes.

2 Meanwhile, in a small bowl mash avocado with a fork. Stir in mayonnaise; set aside.

3 Trim a thin slice off the top of each poblano pepper to remove stem. Remove and discard seeds from inside peppers. For a charcoal or gas grill, place poblano peppers on the grill rack directly over medium heat. Cover and grill for 20 minutes or until peppers are charred and very tender, turning occasionally. Remove from grill and wrap in foil. Let stand for 15 minutes or until cool enough to handle. Using a sharp knife, loosen edges of skins; gently pull off and discard skins. Cut peppers into strips.

4 Divide poblano peppers and cheese among 6 of the chicken patties, being careful to arrange mixture in the center of each patty. Top with remaining patties, pressing edges to seal well.

5 Place patties on grill rack directly over medium heat. Cover and grill for 14 to 18 minutes or until done (165°F),

turning once halfway through grilling. If desired, add buns, cut sides down, to grill the last 2 minutes of grilling or until toasted on one side.

6 Spread cut sides of buns with avocado-mayonnaise spread. Place patties on spread, and, if desired, top with lettuce, tomato, and/or sliced onion.

PER SERVING 632 **CAL**; 41 g **FAT** (12 g **SAT**); 144 mg **CHOL**; 1,126 mg **SODIUM**; 29 g **CARB**; 3 g **FIBER**; 36 g **PRO**

Golden Grilled Chicken Thighs with Apricots

Make these Moroccan-inspired grilled chicken thighs when fresh apricots are in season—generally a brief window in early summer.

MAKES 4 servings   **PREP** 25 minutes   **MARINATE** 2 hours   **GRILL** 12 minutes

1	pound skinless, boneless chicken thighs
	Salt and black pepper
½	cup apricot nectar
5	tablespoons apricot preserves
4	tablespoons snipped fresh mint
1	tablespoon olive oil
1	tablespoon sherry vinegar
½	teaspoon curry powder
1	clove garlic, minced
4	medium apricots, halved and pitted
¼	cup chopped green onions (2)
¼	cup chopped pistachios
1	tablespoon Dijon mustard
1	teaspoon olive oil
½	teaspoon mustard seeds
¼	teaspoon salt

1 Sprinkle chicken with salt and black pepper. Place in a large resealable plastic bag set in a shallow bowl. For marinade, in a small bowl combine ¼ cup of the nectar, 2 tablespoons of the preserves, 2 tablespoons of the mint, the 1 tablespoon olive oil, the vinegar, curry powder, and garlic. Pour over chicken. Seal bag; turn to coat chicken. Marinate in the refrigerator for 2 to 4 hours, turning the bag once or twice.

2 Remove chicken from marinade; discarding marinade. For a charcoal or gas grill, place chicken on the grill rack directly over medium heat. Cover and grill for 12 to 15 minutes or until chicken is no longer pink (180°F), turning once halfway through. Add apricots to grill, cut sides down, the last 5 minutes of grilling or until lightly browned.

3 For sauce, in a small bowl combine the remaining ¼ cup apricot nectar, 3 tablespoons preserves, 2 tablespoons mint, the chopped green onions, 3 tablespoons of the pistachios, the mustard, the 1 teaspoon olive oil, the mustard seeds, and ¼ teaspoon salt. Serve chicken with sauce and apricots; sprinkle with remaining pistachios.

PER SERVING 348 **CAL**; 13 g **FAT** (2 g **SAT**); 94 mg **CHOL**; 504 mg **SODIUM**; 33 g **CARB**; 2 g **FIBER**; 25 g **PRO**

Sesame-Ginger Tuna Steaks

Pineapple is perfectly suited to the grill. The sturdy slices hold up beautifully to the heat—and their intense sweetness and flavor is only improved with a touch of smoke.

MAKES 4 servings   **SOAK** 1 hour   **PREP** 25 minutes   **GRILL** 12 minutes

4	fresh or frozen tuna steaks, 1 to 1½ inches thick
1	14 x 6 x ¾-inch alder or cedar grilling plank
¼	cup bottled plum sauce
1	tablespoon soy sauce
2	teaspoons grated fresh ginger
1	teaspoon rice vinegar
½	teaspoon toasted sesame oil
¼	teaspoon crushed red pepper
1	medium fresh pineapple, peeled, cored, and cut into 8 spears
1	teaspoon sesame seeds and/or black sesame seeds, toasted (see tip, page 47)
	Chopped green onions (optional)

1 Thaw tuna, if frozen. At least 1 hour before grilling, soak plank in enough water to cover. Place a weight on plank so it stays submerged during soaking.

2 For sauce, in a small bowl combine plum sauce, soy sauce, ginger, vinegar, oil, and crushed red pepper; set aside.

3 For a charcoal or gas grill, grease the grill rack. Place plank on the rack of an uncovered grill directly over medium heat for 3 to 5 minutes or until plank begins to crackle and smoke. Meanwhile, grill tuna steaks on the grill rack for 2 to 3 minutes or until grill marks appear. Place tuna steaks, grilled sides up, on plank. Cover and grill for 10 to 15 minutes or until still pink in the center and fish begins to flake easily when tested with a fork. Add pineapple to grill rack during the last 8 to 10 minutes of grilling or until brown, turning occasionally.

4 Transfer tuna and pineapple to a serving platter. Drizzle tuna steaks with sauce; sprinkle with sesame seeds. If desired, sprinkle with green onions.

PER SERVING 292 **CAL**; 2 g **FAT** (1 g **SAT**); 66 mg **CHOL**; 434 mg **SODIUM**; 24 g **CARB**; 2 g **FIBER**; 43 g **PRO**

Grilled Shrimp Panzanella

Panzanella is an Italian salad that was created to use day-old bread. Add a few skewers of grilled shrimp and it becomes a main course for a warm summer night.

MAKES 10 servings   **PREP** 40 minutes   **GRILL** 14 minutes   **CHILL** 1 hour

- 1½ **pounds large fresh or frozen shrimp with tails, peeled and deveined**
- ¾ **cup olive oil**
- ½ **cup white balsamic vinegar or balsamic vinegar**
- 3 **tablespoons lemon juice**
- 2 **cloves garlic, minced**
- ¾ **teaspoon salt**
- ¾ **teaspoon freshly ground black pepper**
- 2 **large red and/or yellow sweet peppers, halved and seeded**
- 2 **medium zucchini, halved lengthwise**
- 1 **1-pound loaf ciabatta bread, cut into 1-inch slices**
- 4 **roma tomatoes, halved**
- ½ **cup coarsely chopped fresh basil (optional)**
- ½ **cup coarsely chopped fresh flat-leaf parsley (optional)**
- ½ **cup Kalamata olives, pitted and halved (optional)**

1 Thaw shrimp, if frozen. For vinaigrette, in a medium bowl combine oil, vinegar, lemon juice, garlic, salt, and black pepper. Thread shrimp onto six 12-inch wooden skewers (see tip, page 11). Brush shrimp with about 3 tablespoons of the vinaigrette; reserve remaining vinaigrette.

2 For a charcoal or gas grill, grease grill rack. Place kabobs on the grill rack directly over medium heat. Cover and grill for 4 minutes or until shrimp are opaque, turning once halfway through grilling. Remove from grill; set aside.

3 Brush sweet peppers and zucchini with some of the vinaigrette; add to grill. Cover and grill for 8 minutes or until crisp-tender and lightly charred, turning once. Remove from grill; set aside.

4 Brush bread slices and tomatoes with some of the vinaigrette; add to grill. Cover and grill for 2 minutes or until bread is lightly toasted and tomatoes are softened, turning once.

5 Remove shrimp from skewers and transfer to an extra-large bowl. Cut sweet peppers, zucchini, and bread into 1-inch pieces; add to bowl. Drizzle with remaining vinaigrette. If desired, add basil, parsley, and olives; toss to combine. Serve immediately or chill for 1 to 2 hours.

PER SERVING 331 **CAL**; 18 g **FAT** (3 g **SAT**); 88 mg **CHOL**; 761 mg **SODIUM**; 29 g **CARB**; 2 g **FIBER**; 14 g **PRO**

Grilled Chile-Lime Shrimp

Shrimp is labeled by the number of shrimp in a pound. For example, shrimp labeled "21/25", means there are between 21 and 25 shrimp in a pound. The smaller the numbers, the bigger the shrimp.

MAKES 4 servings   **PREP** 20 minutes
MARINATE 20 minutes   **GRILL** 4 minutes

1	teaspoon finely shredded lime peel
¼	cup fresh lime juice
1	fresh jalapeño seeded and finely minced (see tip, page 54)
1	tablespoon garlic, minced
2	tablespoons low-sodium soy sauce
3	tablespoons olive oil
1	teaspoon chili powder
¼	teaspoon cayenne pepper
2	tablespoons fresh snipped cilantro
1	tablespoon honey
1½	pounds fresh or frozen medium shrimp in shells (about 10 per person)
	Grilled mango and zucchini slices (optional)

1 For the marinade, in medium bowl combine lime peel, lime juice, jalapeño, garlic, soy sauce, oil, chili powder, cayenne pepper, cilantro, and honey; stir well.

2 Thaw shrimp, if frozen. Peel and devein shrimp, leaving tails intact. Rinse shrimp and pat dry. Place shrimp in a large resealable plastic bag set in a shallow bowl. Pour marinade over shrimp. Seal bag. Through the bag, gently rub marinade into shrimp. Chill for 20 minutes, turning and gently massaging marinade into shrimp halfway through marinating. (Do not marinate longer than 20 minutes because the acidic lime juice will cook the shrimp.)

3 Remove shrimp from marinade; discarding marinade. Place shrimp on cutting board nestled in groups of 10. Using two bamboo skewers (see tip, page 11) for each group, skewer the shrimp.

4 For a charcoal or gas grill, place shrimp kabobs on an oiled grill rack directly over medium-high heat. Cover and grill for 4 minutes or until opaque, turning once halfway through grilling. If desired, serve with grilled mango and zucchini slices.

PER SERVING 211 **CAL**; 6 g **FAT** (1 g **SAT**); 259 mg **CHOL**; 320 mg **SODIUM**; 4 g **CARB**; 35 g **PRO**

Smoked Tomato Po' Boy Sandwiches

The tomatoes are smoked on a hickory or oak grilling plank. Be sure to soak the plank in water for 1 hour before grilling.

MAKES 4 servings   **SOAK** 1 hour   **PREP** 15 minutes
GRILL 10 minutes

1	14 x 6 x ¾-inch hickory or oak grilling plank
2	medium green and/or firm ripe tomatoes (5 to 6 ounces each), cut into ½-inch slices
¼	teaspoon salt
¼	teaspoon black pepper
1	small red onion, cut into ½-inch slices
¼	cup mayonnaise
1	tablespoon pickle relish
1	tablespoon ketchup
2	teaspoons capers
2	teaspoons Creole mustard or spicy brown mustard
2	teaspoons snipped fresh flat-leaf parsley
½	teaspoon bottled hot pepper sauce
4	hoagie buns, split and toasted
1	cup fresh baby arugula or spinach
4	radishes, thinly sliced

1 At least 1 hour before grilling, soak plank in enough water to cover. Place a weight on plank so it stays submerged during soaking.

2 For a charcoal or gas grill, place plank on the rack of a covered grill directly over medium heat. Grill, uncovered, for 3 to 5 minutes or until plank starts to crackle and smoke. Meanwhile, sprinkle tomatoes with salt and black pepper. Turn plank over; place tomato slices on plank. Cover and grill for 10 to 15 minutes or until tomatoes are softened and starting to brown, turning once halfway through grilling. Add onion slices to grill the last 5 to 8 minutes of grilling or until onion is tender, turning once. Remove tomatoes and onion from grill. Separate onion into rings.

3 For remoulade, in a small bowl combine mayonnaise, relish, ketchup, capers, mustard, parsley, and bottled hot pepper sauce. Spread remoulade on cut sides of buns. Fill with arugula, radishes, tomatoes, and onion.

PER SERVING 425 **CAL**; 14 g **FAT** (2 g **SAT**); 5 mg **CHOL**; 951 mg **SODIUM**; 66 g **CARB**; 3 g **FIBER**; 12 g **PRO**

CHAPTER 6

healthy favorites

Delicious low-calorie recipes for eating healthfully.

**PORK TENDERLOIN WITH PAN SAUCE
AND POTATOES**

Cuban Flank Steak-Pepper Soup with Olive Relish

Flank steak is lean, flavorful, and versatile. Grill, broil, stir fry—or simmer in a slow cooker soup, as it is here. The optional olive relish adds a sweet and salty taste to the toasted baguette slices.

MAKES 8 servings   **PREP** 20 minutes   **BROIL** 4 minutes   **SLOW COOK** 8 hours (low)

1½ **pounds flank steak**
1   **tablespoon olive oil**
2   **onions, peeled and diced**
1   **red bell pepper, seeded and diced**
1   **orange bell pepper, seeded and diced**
1   **14- to 15-ounce can no-sodium black beans, rinsed and drained**
1   **cup frozen corn kernels, thawed**
3   **cups reduced-sodium chicken broth**
1   **tablespoon sherry vinegar**
1   **bay leaf**
½   **teaspoon black pepper**
1½ **teaspoons ground cumin**
1   **teaspoon minced garlic**
1   **tablespoon tomato paste**
1   **cup canned diced reduced-salt, fire-roasted tomatoes**
4   **slices baguette, sliced ¼-inch thin and toasted**
¼   **cup Olive Relish (optional)**

1 Preheat broiler to high. Cut flank steak into two crosswise pieces. Brush each piece on both sides with olive oil. Broil, about 4 inches from heat source, for 2 to 3 minutes on each side or until well browned. Transfer steak to a 4-quart slow cooker.

2 Add onions, red bell pepper, orange bell pepper, black beans, corn kernels, chicken broth, sherry vinegar, bay leaf, black pepper, cumin, garlic, tomato paste, and tomatoes.

3 Cover and cook on low-heat setting for 8 hours. Using tongs, remove flank steak from slow cooker and transfer to a cutting board. Using two forks, shred the steak.

4 Ladle soup among four warmed soup bowls. Divide flank steak among the bowls, a pile of shredded steak in the center of each. If desired, spread 1 tablespoon Olive Relish on top of each toasted bread round; place on shredded steak in bowls.

PER SERVING 282 **CAL**; 8 g **FAT** (3 g **SAT**); 55 mg **CHOL**; 388 mg **SODIUM**; 27 g **CARB**; 5 g **FIBER**; 25 g **PRO**

Olive Relish In a small bowl combine ¼ cup drained green olives, coarsely chopped; ¼ cup golden raisins, coarsely chopped; 1 teaspoon capers, drained and rinsed; and 2 teaspoons finely chopped parsley.

Weeknight Boeuf Bourguignon

Serve this classic French stew with a green salad and some crusty bread to sop up the delicious broth flavored with chanterelle mushrooms, garlic, red wine, and herbes de Provence.

MAKES 4 servings   **PREP** 30 minutes   **COOK** 18 minutes

12	ounces boneless beef sirloin steak
1	tablespoon olive oil
1	cup thinly sliced carrots (2 medium)
½	cup thinly sliced celery (1 stalk)
2	cloves garlic, minced
1	cup frozen small whole onions
1	ounce dried chanterelle mushrooms, rinsed and chopped
2¾	cups lower-sodium beef broth
¾	cup dry red wine
½	6-ounce can (⅓ cup) tomato paste
1	teaspoon dried herbes de Provence, crushed
¼	teaspoon ground black pepper
	Snipped fresh parsley
	Cracked black pepper

1 Trim fat from meat. Cut meat into thin bite-size strips. In a 4-quart nonstick Dutch oven heat 2 teaspoons of the oil over medium-high heat. Add meat; cook until browned. Remove meat from Dutch oven. Add the remaining 1 teaspoon oil to Dutch oven; add carrots, celery, and garlic. Cook for 8 to 10 minutes or until vegetables are tender, stirring occasionally. Return meat to Dutch oven; add onions and dried mushrooms.

2 In a medium bowl whisk together broth, wine, tomato paste, herbes de Provence, and pepper until smooth. Stir broth mixture into meat and vegetables. Bring to boiling; reduce heat. Simmer, covered, for 10 minutes to blend flavors. Sprinkle with snipped fresh parsley and cracked black pepper.

PER SERVING 265 **CAL**; 8 g **FAT** (2 g **SAT**); 52 mg **CHOL**; 525 mg **SODIUM**; 17 g **CARB**; 3 g **FIBER**; 22 g **PRO**

Pork Tenderloin with Pan Sauce and Potatoes

Pork tenderloin is lean and—when cut into medallions and pan-fried—quick to prepare. Be sure to scrape all the crusty brown bits from the bottom of the pan. That's what gives rich flavor to the pan sauce.

MAKES 4 servings   **START TO FINISH** 25 minutes

1   **pound pork tenderloin**
⅛   **teaspoon salt**
¼   **teaspoon black pepper**
      Nonstick cooking spray
1½ **cups reduced-sodium chicken broth**
2   **teaspoons cornstarch**
2   **teaspoons Dijon mustard**
2   **cups hot cooked mashed potatoes**
      Snipped fresh chives or sliced green onions (optional)

1 Trim fat from meat. Cut meat into ½-inch slices. Using your hands, gently flatten meat to about ¼-inch thickness. Sprinkle with salt and pepper.

2 Coat an extra-large nonstick skillet with cooking spray; heat skillet over medium heat. Add meat; cook for 3 to 5 minutes or just until pink in center, turning once. Transfer meat to a serving platter; cover to keep warm.

3 Meanwhile, for sauce, in a small bowl stir together broth, cornstarch, and mustard. Add broth to skillet, stirring to scrape up crusty brown bits. Cook and stir over medium heat until slightly thickened and bubbly. Cook and stir for 1 minute more.

4 To serve, spoon sauce over meat and mashed potatoes. If desired, sprinkle with chives.

PER SERVING 252 **CAL**; 7 g **FAT** (3 g **SAT**); 85 mg **CHOL**; 500 mg **SODIUM**; 19 g **CARB**; 2 g **FIBER**; 27 g **PRO**

Garlic Pork with Kale and Walnut Barley

Bags of kale already stemmed, washed, and torn save time in preparing this autumn dish. If you can't find lower-sodium less-fat bacon, opt for center-cut bacon. The sodium won't be any lower, but it is leaner than regular bacon.

MAKES 4 servings   **PREP** 20 minutes   **ROAST** 25 minutes at 425°F   **COOK** 18 minutes   **STAND** 10 minutes

1	**1-pound pork tenderloin**
2	**cloves garlic, minced**
½	**teaspoon dried thyme, crushed**
¼	**teaspoon salt**
¼	**teaspoon black pepper**
3	**strips lower-sodium less-fat bacon, chopped**
3	**cups torn, trimmed fresh kale**
½	**cup walnuts, coarsely chopped**
1	**cup reduced-sodium chicken broth**
⅔	**cup quick-cooking barley**
¼	**cup snipped dried figs**
2	**tablespoons cider vinegar**

1 Preheat oven to 425°F. Trim fat from meat. In a small bowl combine garlic, thyme, salt, and pepper. Sprinkle on pork; rub in with your fingers. Place pork on a rack in a shallow roasting pan.

2 Roast, uncovered, for 25 to 30 minutes or until an instant-read thermometer registers 145°F. Remove pork from pan. Cover; let stand for 10 minutes.

3 Meanwhile, in a large skillet cook bacon over medium heat until it begins to brown. Add kale and walnuts. Cook for 4 to 6 minutes or until bacon is cooked through, walnuts are lightly toasted, and kale is tender. Remove kale mixture from the skillet and set aside.

4 Add broth and barley to the same skillet. Bring to boiling; reduce heat. Cover and simmer for 10 to 12 minutes or until barley is tender, adding figs for the last 1 minute of cooking. Drain, if necessary. Stir in kale mixture and vinegar.

5 Slice pork and serve with Kale and Walnut Barley.

PER SERVING 371 **CAL**; 13 g **FAT** (2 g **SAT**); 76 mg **CHOL**; 406 mg **SODIUM**; 32 g **CARB**; 6 g **FIBER**; 33 g **PRO**

Hungarian-Style Pork Paprikash

Fire-roasted tomatoes impart smoky flavor to this quick paprikash. Intensify that flavor by substituting half the sweet paprika with smoked paprika, if you like.

MAKES 6 servings   **PREP** 15 minutes   **COOK** 15 minutes

- 2 **tablespoons all-purpose flour**
- 1 **tablespoon paprika**
- ¼ **teaspoon black pepper**
- ¼ **teaspoon cayenne pepper**
- 1 **pound pork tenderloin, trimmed and cut into 1-inch cubes**
- 1 **tablespoon olive oil**
- 2 **medium carrots**
- 2 **14.5-ounce cans fire-roasted diced tomatoes**
- 1 **8-ounce can no-salt-added tomato sauce**
- 1 **medium yellow pepper, cut into thin strips (1 cup)**
- 8 **ounces dried whole grain fettuccine**
- ¼ **cup light sour cream or plain Greek fat-free yogurt**
   Snipped fresh flat-leaf parsley (optional)

1 In a resealable plastic bag combine the flour, paprika, black pepper, and cayenne pepper. Add the pork; seal bag. Toss to coat pork with flour mixture. In a large skillet heat oil over medium-high heat. Add pork; cook about 5 minutes or until browned on all sides.

2 Cut carrots in half crosswise. Cut each piece lengthwise into quarters, for a total of 16 carrot sticks. Add carrots, undrained tomatoes, tomato sauce, and yellow pepper to skillet; stir to combine. Bring to boiling; reduce heat. Cover and simmer for 10 minutes, stirring occasionally.

3 Meanwhile, cook pasta according to package directions; drain. Add pasta to pork in skillet; toss to combine. Top each serving with sour cream and, if desired, sprinkle with parsley.

PER SERVING 315 **CAL**; 6 g **FAT** (1 g **SAT**); 52 mg **CHOL**; 379 mg **SODIUM**; 44 g **CARB**; 8 g **FIBER**; 23 g **PRO**

Hot Chicken Salad Casserole

This version of an indulgent potluck favorite swaps low-fat yogurt for traditional mayonnaise and crushed cornflakes for potato-chip topping. The result? Creamy, comforting goodness with far fewer calories and fat grams.

MAKES 6 servings **PREP** 20 minutes **BAKE** 30 minutes at 400°F **STAND** 10 minutes

- **3** cups cubed cooked chicken breast (about 1 pound)
- **1** cup sliced celery (2 stalks)
- **1** cup chopped yellow or red sweet pepper (1 large)
- **¾** cup shredded reduced-fat cheddar or mozzarella cheese (3 ounces)
- **1** 10.75-ounce can reduced-fat and reduced-sodium condensed cream of chicken soup
- **1** 6-ounce carton plain low-fat yogurt
- **¼** cup sliced green onions
- **1** tablespoon lemon juice
- **¼** teaspoon black pepper
- **½** cup crushed cornflakes
- **¼** cup sliced almonds

1 Preheat oven to 400°F. In a large bowl stir together chicken, celery, sweet pepper, cheese, soup, yogurt, green onions, lemon juice, and black pepper. Transfer to a 2-quart rectangular baking dish.

2 In a small bowl stir together cornflakes and almonds. Sprinkle evenly over casserole.

3 Bake, uncovered, for 30 minutes or until heated through. Let stand for 10 minutes before serving.

PER SERVING 251 **CAL**; 9 g **FAT** (4 g **SAT**); 75 mg **CHOL**; 415 mg **SODIUM**; 13 g **CARB**; 2 g **FIBER**; 29 g **PRO**

Lemon-Sage Roasted Chicken Thighs

The chicken thighs are browned in a skillet on the stovetop, then finish roasting in the oven.

MAKES 4 servings **PREP** 30 minutes
BAKE 25 minutes at 375°F

- **8** skinless, boneless chicken thighs (about 2 pounds total)
- **⅛** teaspoon salt
- **¼** teaspoon black pepper
- **2** teaspoons olive oil
- **1** pound baby carrots with ½-inch tops, halved if large
- **4** shallots, quartered
- **3** cloves garlic, thinly sliced
- **1⅓** cups reduced-sodium chicken broth
- **1** teaspoon finely shredded lemon peel
- **2** tablespoons lemon juice
- **1** tablespoon all-purpose flour
- **¼** cup dry white wine
- **2** tablespoons snipped fresh sage
  Lemon wedges

1 Preheat oven to 375°F. Season chicken with salt and pepper. In an extra-large ovenproof skillet cook chicken in hot oil over medium-high heat about 5 minutes or until browned, turning once. Add carrots, shallots, and garlic to skillet. Pour ⅓ cup of the chicken broth and the lemon juice over chicken in skillet. Bring to boiling.

2 Place skillet in oven; roast, uncovered, about 25 minutes or just until chicken is done (180°F) and carrots are tender. Transfer chicken and carrots to a platter, cover with foil to keep warm.

3 Whisk flour into remaining broth. Add broth mixture and wine to the hot skillet. Whisk to combine. Return skillet to medium-high heat. Cook and stir to scrape up any browned bits from the bottom of the pan. Bring to boiling. Boil gently, uncovered, about 5 minutes or until liquid is slightly thickened and reduced to about ½ cup. Stir in sage and lemon peel. Serve sauce with chicken and carrots. Serve with lemon wedges.

PER SERVING 376 **CAL**; 11 g **FAT** (3 g **SAT**); 215 mg **CHOL**; 297 mg **SODIUM**; 18 g **CARB**; 5 g **FIBER**; 47 g **PRO**

Barbecue Chicken Pot Pie

Barbecue chicken pizza is one of the most popular pizzas in the country, so why not a BBQ chicken pot pie?

MAKES 6 servings **PREP** 45 minutes
BAKE 15 minutes at 450°F **STAND** 5 minutes

- **½** pound sweet potatoes or Yukon gold potatoes, peeled and cut into ¾-inch cubes
- **¼** teaspoon salt
- **½** cup chopped parsnips or carrots
- **1¼** pounds skinless, boneless chicken thighs, cut into ¾-inch pieces
- **2** teaspoons olive oil
- **½** cup chopped onion (1 medium)
- **½** cup chopped celery (1 stalk)
- **1** 8-ounce package sliced button mushrooms
- **⅔** cup barbecue sauce
- **½** 14.1-ounce package rolled refrigerated unbaked piecrust (1 crust)
- **1** egg
- **1** tablespoon water

1 Preheat oven to 450°F. In a medium saucepan combine potatoes and ¼ teaspoon salt; add enough water to cover. Bring to boiling; reduce heat. Cover; simmer for 10 to 12 minutes or just until tender. Add parsnips to the potatoes during the last 4 minutes of cooking. Drain; cool slightly.

2 Meanwhile, in an extra large skillet cook chicken in hot oil over medium heat about 5 minutes or until browned, stirring occasionally. Remove chicken from skillet; set aside. Add onion, celery, and mushrooms to skillet. Cook and stir about 10 minutes or until vegetables are tender. Return chicken to skillet. Stir in barbecue sauce and cooked potatoes and parsnips. Heat through. Divide evenly among six 10-ounce ramekins or custard cups. Set aside.

3 Unroll piecrust. Press or roll piecrust into a 12-inch circle. Cut crust into ½-inch-wide strips. Cut long center strips in half. Arrange half the strips 1 inch apart on filling (about three per ramekin). Arrange remaining strips perpendicular to the first strips (about three per ramekin).

4 In a small bowl whisk together the egg and water. Brush egg mixture on lattice crusts.

5 Bake, uncovered, for 15 to 20 minutes or until filling is bubbly and crust is golden brown. Let stand for 5 minutes.

PER SERVING 369 **CAL**; 14 g **FAT** (4 g **SAT**); 97 mg **CHOL**; 600 mg **SODIUM**; 38 g **CARB**; 3 g **FIBER**; 22 g **PRO**

BARBECUE CHICKEN POT PIE

Italian Chicken Sandwich

With the skin removed, chicken thighs are actually low in fat and have the benefit of being juicier and more flavorful than skinless chicken breasts.

MAKES 4 servings   **PREP** 30 minutes   **COOK** 3 minutes

12	**ounces skinless, boneless chicken thighs, cut into thin strips**
1	**teaspoon dried Italian seasoning, crushed**
2	**teaspoons olive oil**
¾	**cup green sweet pepper strips (1 medium)**
¾	**cup red sweet pepper strips (1 medium)**
¾	**cup thinly sliced onion (1 medium)**
⅔	**cup light roasted red pepper-and-garlic-flavor pasta sauce**
4	**rosemary-and-olive-oil-flavor foldable flatbreads**
½	**cup shredded part-skim mozzarella cheese**
¼	**cup coarsely chopped mild banana peppers**
2	**tablespoons snipped fresh basil**

1 Season chicken with Italian seasoning. In a large nonstick skillet cook chicken in hot oil over medium heat about 5 minutes or just until browned. Stir in green pepper, red pepper, and onion. Cook for 5 to 7 minutes or just until vegetables are tender. Stir in pasta sauce; heat through.

2 Spoon chicken mixture evenly onto one side of each flatbread. Sprinkle with mozzarella cheese, banana peppers, and basil. Fold flatbreads in half (sandwiches will be full).

3 Preheat a covered indoor grill, panini press, grill pan, or large skillet. Place sandwiches, half at a time, in grill. Cover and cook 3 to 4 minutes or until browned and cheese is melted. (If using a grill pan or skillet, place sandwiches on grill pan or skillet. Weight sandwiches down* and cook for 2 to 3 minutes or until bread is toasted. Turn sandwiches over, weight down, and cook about 2 minutes more or until toasted and cheese is melted.)

***Tip** Weight the sandwiches down by placing a heavy skillet on top of them; add unopened cans of food to the top skillet. (If you use a heavy cast-iron skillet, you might not need to use cans for weight.)

PER SERVING 309 **CAL**; 10 g **FAT** (3 g **SAT**); 90 mg **CHOL**; 577 mg **SODIUM**; 31 g **CARB**; 6 g **FIBER**; 27 g **PRO**

Shrimp, Scallops, and Pineapple Kabobs with Cilantro Aïoli

Traditional aïoli is nearly all full-fat mayonnaise. This lightened version is made with equal parts light mayonnaise and fat-free sour cream spiked with a generous dose of garlic, cilantro, and a hot chile.

MAKES 8 servings   **PREP** 35 minutes   **MARINATE** 30 minutes   **GRILL** 5 minutes

1	pound fresh or frozen peeled and deveined large shrimp (tails left on)
1	pound fresh or frozen sea scallops
3	tablespoons lime juice
1	tablespoon vegetable oil or canola oil
1	teaspoon garlic powder
1	teaspoon ground coriander
1	teaspoon sweet paprika
1	teaspoon Asian chili sauce (Sriracha sauce)
½	teaspoon ground black pepper
¾	fresh pineapple, peeled, cored, and cut into 1½-inch pieces (about 3 cups)
6	cloves garlic, minced
1	teaspoon olive oil
½	cup finely snipped fresh cilantro
¼	cup light mayonnaise
¼	cup fat-free sour cream
1	fresh serrano chile pepper or jalapeño chile pepper, stemmed, seeded, and finely chopped (see tip, page 54)

1 Thaw shrimp and scallops, if frozen. Rinse shrimp and scallops; pat dry with paper towels.

2 In a large bowl whisk together 2 tablespoons of the lime juice, the vegetable oil, garlic powder, coriander, paprika, chili sauce, and black pepper. Add shrimp, scallops, and pineapple, tossing gently to coat. Cover and marinate in the refrigerator 30 minutes.

3 Meanwhile, for Cilantro Aïoli, in a medium microwave-safe bowl stir together garlic and olive oil. Microwave on high 20 seconds; stir. Microwave 20 seconds more, watching closely to avoid burning garlic. Stir in cilantro, mayonnaise, sour cream, chile pepper, and the remaining 1 tablespoon lime juice. Cover and chill until serving time.

4 Using sixteen 12-inch skewers (see tip, page 11) , two for each kabob, place skewers in pairs, parallel to one another. Alternately thread shrimp, scallops, and pineapple on the parallel skewers, dividing ingredients evenly among skewers and leaving ¼ inch between pieces. For a charcoal or gas grill, place kabobs on a greased grill rack directly over medium heat. Cover and grill for 5 to 8 minutes or until shrimp and scallops are opaque, turning once halfway through grilling. Serve with Cilantro Aïoli.

PER SERVING 183 **CAL**; 7 g **FAT** (1 g **SAT**); 88 mg **CHOL**; 600 mg **SODIUM**; 14 g **CARB**; 1 g **FIBER**; 15 g **PRO**

Pacific Northwest Paella

Inspired by the national dish of Spain—a combination of fish, shellfish, chicken, and sausages—this American version calls for popular Pacific Northwest ingredients, including salmon, mushrooms, and asparagus.

MAKES 6 servings   **START TO FINISH** 45 minutes

1¼   **pounds fresh or frozen skinless salmon fillets, about 1 inch thick**

4   **slices apple wood-smoked bacon**

3   **cups sliced fresh cremini or button mushrooms (8 ounces)**

1   **cup chopped onion (1 large)**

2   **cloves garlic, minced**

2½   **cups chicken broth**

1   **cup uncooked long grain white rice**

2   **teaspoons snipped fresh thyme or ½ teaspoon dried thyme, crushed**

¼   **teaspoon cracked black pepper**

1   **pound fresh asparagus, trimmed and cut into 1-inch pieces, or one 10-ounce package frozen cut asparagus, thawed**

⅓   **cup chopped roma tomato (1 medium)**

1 Thaw fish, if frozen. In a large deep skillet or paella pan cook bacon over medium heat until crisp. Remove bacon and drain on paper towels, reserving drippings in skillet. Crumble bacon; set aside.

2 Add mushrooms, onion, and garlic to the reserved drippings. Cook about 5 minutes or until onion is tender, stirring occasionally. Stir in broth, rice, and thyme. Bring to boiling; reduce heat. Simmer, covered, for 10 minutes.

3 Meanwhile, rinse fish; pat dry with paper towels. Cut fish into 1-inch pieces. Sprinkle with pepper; toss gently.

4 Place fish and asparagus on the rice mixture. Simmer, covered, for 10 to 12 minutes or until fish begins to flake when tested with a fork and asparagus is crisp-tender. Sprinkle with chopped tomato and crumbled bacon.

PER SERVING 313 **CAL**; 9 g **FAT** (2 g **SAT**); 60 mg **CHOL**; 498 mg **SODIUM**; 32 g **CARB**; 2 g **FIBER**; 26 g **PRO**

Linguine in Fresh Tomato Sauce with Garlic-Basil Toast

The cherry tomatoes are cooked just until they are softened and juicy in this light dish that suits a warm summer evening.

MAKES 4 servings   **START TO FINISH** 25 minutes

10	ounces dried linguine
3	tablespoons olive oil
1	tablespoon minced garlic (6 cloves)
2	English muffins, split
¾	cup snipped fresh basil
2¼	cups cherry tomatoes, halved
1	teaspoon sugar
	Salt
	Black pepper
½	cup pitted Kalamata olives, halved
	Grated Parmesan cheese (optional)
	Snipped fresh basil (optional)

1 Preheat broiler. Cook pasta in boiling, lightly salted water according to package directions. Using a ladle remove ½ cup of cooking water; set aside. Drain pasta. Return pasta to hot pan; cover and keep warm.

2 Meanwhile, in a small bowl combine 1 tablespoon of the oil and about 1 teaspoon of the minced garlic. Brush on cut sides of muffins. Place muffins on a baking sheet. Broil 3 to 4 inches from heat for 2 to 3 minutes or until golden and toasted. Sprinkle with 1 tablespoon of the snipped basil; set aside.

3 For sauce, in large saucepan heat the remaining 2 tablespoons oil over medium-high. Add the remaining 2 teaspoons garlic, the remaining basil, and the tomatoes. Cook for 2 minutes; add the reserved ½ cup pasta cooking water and the sugar. Cook for 3 to 4 minutes more or until tomatoes have softened. Season to taste with salt and pepper. Add pasta and olives to sauce; stir to combine and heat through.

4 If desired, sprinkle with Parmesan cheese and top with basil. Serve with toasted muffins.

PER SERVING 448 **CAL**; 12 g **FAT** (2 g **SAT**); 0 mg **CHOL**; 429 mg **SODIUM**; 72 g **CARB**; 3 g **FIBER**; 12 g **PRO**

Four-Cheese Macaroni and Cheese

Butternut squash bulks up the volume and nutrition in this golden, gooey mac and cheese.

MAKES 8 servings **PREP** 30 minutes **ROAST** 40 minutes **BAKE** 25 minutes at 375°F

Nonstick cooking spray
- 1 **pound butternut squash, halved and seeded**
- 8 **ounces dried whole grain elbow macaroni (about 2 cups)**
- 4 **teaspoons butter**
- 2 **tablespoons all-purpose flour**
- ½ **teaspoon salt**
- ⅛ **teaspoon ground white pepper**
- 1 **cup fat-free milk**
- 2 **tablespoons semisoft cheese with garlic and fine herbs**
- ¾ **cup shredded part-skim mozzarella cheese (3 ounces)**
- ¾ **cup shredded reduced-fat sharp cheddar cheese (3 ounces)**
- 2 **ounces Muenster cheese, thinly sliced**

1 Preheat oven to 375°F. Line a 15×10×1-inch baking pan with parchment paper; set aside. Coat a 2-quart square baking dish with cooking spray; set aside.

2 Coat cut sides of squash with cooking spray; place squash, cut sides down, on the prepared baking sheet. Roast for 40 to 45 minutes or until very tender. Let stand until cool enough to handle. Scoop flesh from squash halves; discard skin. Using a potato masher, mash the squash; set aside.

3 Meanwhile, cook pasta according to package directions. Drain well.

4 In a large saucepan melt butter over medium heat. Whisk in the flour, salt, and pepper until combined. Whisk in milk until smooth; cook and stir until thickened and bubbly. Add semisoft cheese; whisk until cheese is melted. Stir in squash. Add cooked pasta; stir until coated.

5 Place half the pasta mixture in the prepared baking dish. Evenly sprinkle half the mozzarella cheese and half the cheddar cheese on the pasta. Arrange half the Muenster cheese over all. Repeat layers. Bake, uncovered, for 25 minutes or until cheese is bubbly and golden brown.

PER SERVING 263 **CAL**; 11 g **FAT** (6 g **SAT**); 29 mg **CHOL**; 403 mg **SODIUM**; 30 g **CARB**; 4 g **FIBER**; 13 g **PRO**

Warm Weather Watermelon and Lentil Gazpacho

The star ingredient—lentils—adds texture to this refreshing cold soup that won Margee Berry of White Salmon, Washington, the top prize of $2,000 at the 2014 Legendary Lentil Cook-Off at the 26th Annual National Lentil Festival in Pullman, Washington. Living in the Northwest, Margee says, provides a "wonderful bounty" of fresh ingredients. Watermelon adds sweetness and chipotle a spicy kick to the traditional gazpacho ingredients of tomato and cucumber.

MAKES 6 servings   **PREP** 20 minutes   **CHILL** 1 hour

4	cups cubed peeled seedless watermelon
1	cup cubed cucumber
1	medium roma tomato
¼	cup fresh lime juice
2	green onions, coarsely chopped
1	small fresh jalapeño, seeded and coarsely chopped (see tip, page 54)
2	tablespoons coarsely chopped fresh mint
1	tablespoon tomato paste
1	teaspoon bottled chipotle pepper sauce
½	teaspoon salt
½	teaspoon ground cumin
⅓	cup coarsely chopped cilantro
1½	cups cooked USA-grown lentils

1 In a food processor place watermelon, cucumber, tomato, lime juice, green onions, jalapeño, mint, tomato paste, hot sauce, salt, and cumin. Add all but 1 tablespoon of the cilantro. Process until smooth. Transfer to a large bowl and stir in lentils. Cover and chill soup in the refrigerator 1 hour or until cold. To serve, ladle soup into bowls and garnish with remaining cilantro.

Tip For best results, chill the produce in this recipe before cutting and placing in the food processor.

PER SERVING 102 **CAL**; 0 g **FAT** (0 g **SAT**); 0 mg **CHOL**; 240 mg **SODIUM**; 21 g **CARB**; 5 g **FIBER**; 6 g **PRO**

CHAPTER 7

potluck pleasers

Take some fresh new ideas and dishes to your next potluck gathering.

SOUTHERN FRIED CHICKEN
DINNER IN A BOWL

Mediterranean Brisket

The first time Dinah Hendon of Verona, New Jersey, made brisket for dinner guests—years ago—it was so dry she was nearly in tears in her kitchen, with company in the dining room. Dinah has obviously gotten her technique down since then. Her tender, juicy brisket, featuring sun-dried tomatoes, garnered her the $2,500 grand prize in the 2014 Mooney Farms Bella Sun Luci recipe contest. Dinah—a first-time recipe contest competitor—combined two brisket recipes and added a few twists of her own to create this winning dish.

MAKES 10 servings **PREP** 30 minutes **COOK** 22 minutes **BAKE** 3 hours at 350°F **STAND** 15 minutes

5	to 6 pounds first cut (flat cut) fresh beef brisket
2	teaspoons all-purpose flour
	Salt
	Coarse ground black pepper
¼	cup Bella Sun Luci® extra-virgin olive oil
3	tablespoons tomato paste
6	large onions, sliced into ¼-inch slices (6 cups)
2	medium red sweet peppers, seeded and sliced into rings, ¼-inch wide
1	15-ounce can plum tomatoes
1	to 2 cups beef broth
3	medium carrots cut into ½-inch pieces (1½ cups)
1	8.5-ounce jar Bella Sun Luci Sun-Dried Tomato Halves®, drained and cut into quarters

1 Preheat oven to 350°F. Sprinkle the brisket with flour, salt, and pepper. In an 8-quart Dutch oven heat oil over medium heat. Add the brisket and brown for 5 minutes on each side. Remove brisket from Dutch oven. Spread the fatty side of the brisket with tomato paste; set aside.

2 Add the onions to the Dutch oven and cook for 8 to 12 minutes or until onions are tender, scraping up the browned bits from the bottom of the Dutch oven with a wooden spoon. Add red sweet peppers and cook 4 to 6 minutes or until peppers are beginning to soften and onions are beginning to brown.

3 Drain and coarsely chop the plum tomatoes, reserving the juices. Add enough beef broth to the reserved juices to equal 2 cups.

4 Add carrots, plum tomatoes, dried tomatoes, and reserved liquid to the Dutch oven. Bring to boiling. Place the brisket on the carrots and tomatoes. Cover with lid.

5 Bake brisket for 3 to 3½ hours or until meat is tender.

6 Transfer brisket to a cutting board. Remove excess fat, if desired. Let stand for 15 minutes. Slice the meat across the grain. Serve with vegetables. Skim fat from cooking juices and drizzle servings with some of the cooking liquid.

PER SERVING 701 **CAL**; 46 g **FAT** (16 g **SAT**); 198 mg **CHOL**; 725 mg **SODIUM**; 26 g **CARB**; 6 g **FIBER**; 46 g **PRO**

Overnight Breakfast Pie

Whether you take this cheesy hash brown-bacon-egg dish for a breakfast gathering or another meal, count on taking an empty dish home.

MAKES 6 servings **PREP** 20 minutes **CHILL** 2 hours **BAKE** 50 minutes at 325°F

8	slices bacon
½	cup panko bread crumbs
5	eggs
2½	cups frozen shredded hash brown potatoes
1	cup shredded Swiss cheese (4 ounces)
½	cup cottage cheese
⅓	cup milk
¼	cup chopped green onions (2)
½	teaspoon salt
¼	teaspoon black pepper
4	drops bottled hot pepper sauce
	Sliced green onions (optional)

1 In a large skillet cook bacon over medium heat until crisp. Drain bacon on paper towels, reserving 1 tablespoon drippings in skillet. Crumble bacon; set aside. Stir bread crumbs into the reserved drippings in skillet. Transfer to a small bowl; cover and chill until needed.

2 Lightly grease a 9-inch pie plate; set aside. In a medium bowl beat eggs with a fork until foamy. Stir in crumbled bacon, hash brown potatoes, Swiss cheese, cottage cheese, milk, the ¼ cup green onions, the salt, black pepper, and hot pepper sauce. Pour into prepared pie plate. Cover and chill for 2 to 24 hours.

3 Preheat oven to 325°F. Sprinkle pie with bread crumb mixture. Bake, uncovered, for 50 minutes or until a knife inserted in the center comes out clean. If desired, sprinkle pie with additional sliced green onions.

PER SERVING 325 **CAL**; 18 g **FAT** (8 g **SAT**); 211 mg **CHOL**; 642 mg **SODIUM**; 22 g **CARB**; 2 g **FIBER**; 19 g **PRO**

Braised Beef and Biscuit Pie

Buttery homemade biscuits flavored with sharp cheddar cheese crown this bubbling beef casserole. It's hearty and warming—just right for a cold winter night.

MAKES 10 to 12 servings   **PREP** 30 minutes   **COOK** 1 hour 6 minutes   **BAKE** 25 minutes at 400°F

3	pounds beef stew meat, cut into 1-inch pieces
1	14.5-ounce can petite diced tomatoes
1	cup chopped onion (1 large)
½	cup tomato paste
⅓	cup dry red wine or beef broth
⅓	cup beef broth
2	tablespoons balsamic vinegar
6	cloves garlic, minced
1	teaspoon dried rosemary, crushed
½	teaspoon salt
½	teaspoon black pepper
12	ounces assorted fresh mushrooms, sliced
1	tablespoon olive oil
1	recipe Cheddar Biscuit Topping

1 In a 4-quart Dutch oven combine stew meat, tomatoes, onion, tomato paste, wine, broth, balsamic vinegar, garlic, rosemary, salt, and pepper. Bring to boiling; reduce heat. Cover and simmer for 1 to 1½ hours or until meat is tender, stirring occasionally.

2 Meanwhile, in a large skillet cook mushrooms in hot oil over medium-high heat for 6 to 8 minutes or until golden brown, stirring occasionally. Stir into cooked meat mixture.

3 Preheat oven to 400°F. Transfer meat mixture to a 3-quart casserole. Prepare Cheddar Biscuit Topper. On a lightly floured surface roll biscuit dough from the center to edges to ½-inch thickness. Cut 2-inch rounds from the dough, rerolling scraps as necessary. Arrange dough on filling. Brush tops with milk. Place casserole on a sturdy baking sheet.

4 Bake, uncovered, for 25 to 30 minutes or until biscuits are golden brown and casserole is bubbly.

Cheddar Biscuit Topping In a large bowl combine 1½ cups all-purpose flour, 1 teaspoon baking powder, and ¼ teaspoon salt. Using a pastry blender, cut in ⅓ cup butter until mixture resembles coarse crumbs. In a small bowl beat together ⅓ cup buttermilk and 1 egg. Add buttermilk mixture all at once to flour mixture. Using a fork, stir just until dough is moistened. Stir in ½ cup shredded sharp cheddar cheese (2 ounces). Using floured hands, gently knead dough in bowl until it holds together.

PER SERVING 445 **CAL**; 22 g **FAT** (10 g **SAT**); 119 mg **CHOL**; 636 mg **SODIUM**; 23 g **CARB**; 2 g **FIBER**; 36 g **PRO**

Roasted Tomato and Bacon Cobbler

Andria Gaskins of Matthews, North Carolina, turned a favorite recipe for tomato pie upside down to create this dish that earned the first-place prize of $5,000 in the 2014 National Cornbread Festival Cook-Off sponsored by Martha White®, Lodge® Manufacturing, and Brown® Stone Works, Inc. "What's an upside-down tomato pie? "A cobbler!" Andria says. The judges obviously liked the reversal as well.

MAKES 8 servings   **PREP** 25 minutes   **ROAST** 30 minutes at 450°F   **COOK** 15 minutes   **BAKE** 32 minutes at 425°F   **STAND** 5 minutes

2¼ **pounds roma tomatoes, cut into ½-inch thick slices**
2 **tablespoons Crisco® extra-virgin olive oil**
1 **teaspoon kosher salt**
1 **teaspoon sugar**
¾ **teaspoon coarse ground black pepper**
1 **tablespoon Crisco® vegetable oil**
1 **medium sweet onion, thinly sliced**
1 **cup shredded sharp cheddar cheese**
1 **cup shredded Havarti cheese**
½ **cup mayonnaise**
¼ **cup Parmesan cheese**
¼ **cup chopped dried tomatoes (not oil-packed)**
¼ **cup sliced fresh basil leaves**
¼ **cup chopped fresh parsley**
¼ **teaspoon crushed red pepper**
1 **7-ounce package Martha White® yellow cornbread and muffin mix**
4 **slices thick cut bacon, cooked and crumbled**
2 **tablespoons chopped dried tomatoes (not oil-packed)**
⅔ **cup milk**

1 For roasted tomatoes, preheat oven to 450°F. Line a 15×10×1-inch baking pan with foil and brush with 1 tablespoon of the olive oil. Place tomatoes on the pan in a single layer; brush with remaining 1 tablespoon olive oil. Sprinkle with salt, sugar, and black pepper. Roast for 25 to 30 minutes or until tomatoes are browned. Reduce oven temperature to 425°F.

2 For caramelized onions, in a 10½-inch Lodge® cast-iron skillet heat the 1 tablespoon vegetable oil over medium-low heat. Add onion and cook 15 minutes or until golden, stirring frequently. Set aside to cool. In a medium bowl combine cheddar, Havarti, mayonnaise, Parmesan, ¼ cup dried tomatoes, the basil, 2 tablespoons of the parsley, and crushed red pepper. Stir in caramelized onions. Arrange half the tomatoes in skillet. Spread with cheese mixture. Layer remaining tomatoes over cheese mixture. Bake for 20 minutes.

3 For the cobbler, in a medium bowl stir together cornbread and muffin mix, bacon, 2 tablespoons dried tomatoes, the remaining 2 tablespoons parsley, and the milk. Pour batter evenly over tomatoes. Bake for 12 to 17 minutes or until golden brown. Let stand 5 minutes before serving.

PER SERVING 402 **CAL**; 27 g **FAT** (9 g **SAT**); 38 mg **CHOL**; 792 mg **SODIUM**; 28 g **CARB**; 2 g **FIBER**; 12 g **PRO**

Chicken Salad with Dried Apricots, Hazelnuts, and Feta with Greek Yogurt Dressing

For the cooked chicken breast, bake bone-in breasts (with skin) at 400°F for 35 to 40 minutes or until the internal temperature reaches 165°F. Cool completely then remove skin before cutting into cubes.

MAKES 8 servings   **START TO FINISH** 40 minutes

2	**cups plain Greek yogurt**
½	**cup honey**
2	**tablespoons snipped fresh mint**
1	**teaspoon finely shredded orange peel**
½	**teaspoon salt**
¼	**teaspoon black pepper**
2	**tablespoons milk (optional)**
2½	**to 3 pounds cooked chicken breast, cut into 1-inch cubes (about 6½ cups)**
1	**cup crumbled feta cheese (4 ounces)**
1	**cup quartered dried apricots**
1	**cup coarsely chopped hazelnuts, toasted***

Lettuce leaves
Crumbled feta cheese (optional)
Snipped dried apricots (optional)
Toasted hazelnuts*, chopped (optional)
Snipped fresh mint (optional)

1 In a large bowl whisk together the yogurt, honey, snipped mint, orange peel, salt, and pepper. If needed, add milk, 1 tablespoon at a time, to reach desired consistency.

2 In an extra-large bowl combine chicken, feta, apricots and, hazelnuts. Add yogurt mixture; mix well. Serve immediately or cover and chill up to 2 hours.

3 Serve salad on a platter lined with lettuce leaves. If desired, sprinkle with additional crumbled feta, dried apricots, hazelnuts, and fresh mint.

*Tip To toast hazelnuts, preheat oven to 350°F. Spread nuts in a single layer in a shallow baking pan. Bake for 8 to 10 minutes or until lightly toasted, stirring once to toast evenly. Cool nuts slightly. Place the warm nuts on a clean kitchen towel; rub with towel to remove the loose skins.

PER SERVING 687 **CAL**; 27 g **FAT** (11 g **SAT**); 148 mg **CHOL**; 714 mg **SODIUM**; 54 g **CARB**; 4 g **FIBER**; 57 g **PRO**

Southern Fried Chicken Dinner in a Bowl

It's all here in one big bowl—crispy chicken, crunchy coleslaw, barbecue beans, and cornbread. Using prepared breaded chicken breasts and bakery corn muffins keeps the dish easy.

MAKES 10 servings **PREP** 30 minutes **CHILL** 2 hours **BAKE** 16 minutes at 375°F

4	cups shredded cabbage*
1	cup shredded carrots (2 medium)*
¼	cup thinly sliced green onions (2)
½	cup mayonnaise
2	tablespoons sugar
1	tablespoon lemon juice
¼	teaspoon salt
¼	teaspoon ground white pepper
12	purchased mini corn muffins, halved, or 6 regular size homemade or purchased corn muffins
¼	cup butter, melted
14	ounces frozen cooked, breaded chicken breast fillets, prepared according to package directions
1	15.5- to 22-ounce can barbecue beans
1½	cups chopped green, yellow, and/or red tomatoes (2 large)
¾	cup bottled ranch salad dressing

1 For slaw, in a large bowl combine cabbage, carrots, and green onions; toss to mix. For dressing, in a small bowl stir together mayonnaise, sugar, lemon juice, salt, and pepper. Add dressing to cabbage mixture; toss to combine. Cover and chill for 2 hours, stirring occasionally.

2 Meanwhile, preheat oven to 375°F. Cut corn muffins into 1-inch cubes. Place cubes in a large shallow baking pan; drizzle with melted butter; toss to coat. Bake for 16 to 18 minutes or until crisp, stirring twice. Set aside.

3 Transfer slaw to two extra-large salad bowls. Cut chicken into strips. Arrange chicken strips, beans, tomatoes, and corn muffins over slaw. If desired, cover and chill up to 6 hours.

4 Just before serving, spoon ranch dressing over all.

* If desired, substitute 5 cups packaged shredded cabbage with carrot (coleslaw mix) for cabbage and carrots.

PER SERVING 482 **CAL**; 32 g **FAT** (8 g **SAT**); 51 mg **CHOL**; 886 mg **SODIUM**; 39 g **CARB**; 5 g **FIBER**; 11 g **PRO**

Smoked Chicken and Asparagus Strata with Dill Havarti

This elegant strata is bit like a savory bread pudding. Serve at brunch or as a supper dish. Look for smoked chicken in the deli department of your supermarket—or wherever rotisserie chickens are sold.

MAKES 12 servings   **PREP** 30 minutes   **CHILL** 2 hours   **STAND** 15 minutes   **BAKE** 50 minutes at 350°F

2	tablespoons butter
½	cup finely chopped onion (1 medium)
⅓	cup finely chopped red sweet pepper
8	ounces asparagus spears, trimmed and cut into 1-inch pieces
¼	cup chicken broth
4	cups cubed smoked chicken or turkey
¾	cup light mayonnaise
6	eggs, lightly beaten
1¼	cups milk
1¼	cups chicken broth
2	tablespoons snipped fresh chives
2	tablespoons country Dijon mustard
½	teaspoon salt
½	teaspoon black pepper
8	cups garlic and herb Italian flatbread (focaccia) cubes
1½	cups shredded Havarti cheese with dill (6 ounces)

1 In a large skillet melt butter over medium-high heat. Add onion and sweet pepper; cook for 3 minutes, stirring occasionally. Add asparagus and ¼ cup broth. Simmer, covered, for 3 minutes or until asparagus is crisp-tender. Transfer vegetables to a large bowl; cool slightly. Stir in smoked chicken and mayonnaise; set aside.

2 In a medium bowl combine eggs, milk, 1¼ cups broth, chives, mustard, salt, and black pepper.

3 Lightly grease a 3-quart rectangular baking dish. Spread half the bread cubes in the prepared baking dish; top evenly with chicken mixture. Spread remaining bread cubes over chicken mixture. Pour egg mixture evenly over layers in dish. Cover and chill for 2 to 24 hours.

4 Before baking, let strata stand at room temperature for 15 minutes. Preheat oven to 350°F. Bake, uncovered, for 40 to 45 minutes or until set and light brown. Sprinkle with cheese. Bake for 10 minutes or until cheese is melted.

PER SERVING 281 **CAL**; 16 g **FAT** (6 g **SAT**); 158 mg **CHOL**; 1,215 mg **SODIUM**; 14 g **CARB**; 1 g **FIBER**; 20 g **PRO**

Spicy Shrimp with Cabbage-Noodle Slaw

This Asian-style slaw is a combination of complementary temperatures and textures—warm, tender shrimp plus noodles tossed with cool, crunchy vegetables.

MAKES 8 servings   **PREP** 35 minutes   **COOK** 3 minutes

- 1½ **pounds fresh or frozen peeled, deveined large shrimp**
- 1 **tablespoon vegetable oil**
- 4 **cloves garlic, minced**
- 1 **teaspoon crushed red pepper**
- 4 **ounces dried rice vermicelli**
- 4 **cups shredded napa cabbage**
- 1 **cup shredded bok choy**
- 1 **cup coarsely shredded carrots (2 medium)**
- ½ **cup thinly sliced radishes**
- ½ **cup bite-size strips cucumber**
- ½ **cup bite-size strips red sweet pepper (1 small)**
- ¼ **cup snipped fresh cilantro**
- 1 **recipe Lime-Ginger Dressing**
- ¼ **cup sliced almonds, toasted (see tip, page 47)**

1 Thaw shrimp, if frozen. Rinse shrimp and pat dry with paper towels.

2 In a large skillet heat vegetable oil over medium heat. Add garlic and crushed red pepper; cook and stir for 30 seconds. Add shrimp; cook and stir for 3 to 4 minutes or until shrimp are opaque. Remove from heat; set aside.

3 Meanwhile, cook noodles in lightly salted boiling water for 3 minutes; drain. Use kitchen scissors to snip noodles into smaller pieces. Set aside.

4 In an extra-large bowl combine cabbage, bok choy, carrots, radishes, cucumber, sweet pepper, cilantro, and drained rice noodles. Pour Lime-Ginger Dressing over cabbage slaw; toss gently to coat. Transfer slaw to platter; top with shrimp. Sprinkle with almonds.

Lime-Ginger Dressing In a small bowl whisk together 3 tablespoons vegetable oil, 2 tablespoons lime juice, 2 tablespoons rice vinegar, 2 teaspoons grated fresh ginger, 2 teaspoons honey, 2 teaspoons soy sauce, ½ teaspoon salt, and ¼ teaspoon cayenne pepper.

PER SERVING 249 **CAL**; 10 g **FAT** (1 g **SAT**); 129 mg **CHOL**; 405 mg **SODIUM**; 20 g **CARB**; 2 g **FIBER**; 20 g **PRO**

Macaroni with Mushrooms and Blue Cheese

A sophisticated take on mac and cheese, this rich dish features chewy pasta swathed in a sauce of tangy blue cheese, mushrooms and baby spinach—and a topping of toasty walnuts.

MAKES 8 servings   **PREP** 30 minutes   **BAKE** 15 minutes at 350°F

Nonstick cooking spray
1   pound dried cavatappi, elbow macaroni, or dried bow tie pasta (4 cups)
1   tablespoon olive oil
8   ounces fresh white, brown, and/or shiitake mushrooms, sliced
½   cup chopped onion (1 medium)
3   cloves garlic, minced
4   cups fresh baby spinach
2   tablespoons butter
2   tablespoons all-purpose flour
¼   teaspoon ground nutmeg
¼   teaspoon black pepper
1½   cups whole milk
1¼   cups crumbed blue cheese or Gorgonzola (5 ounces)
½   cup chopped walnuts, toasted (see tip, page 47)

1 Preheat oven to 350°F. Coat a 2-quart baking dish with cooking spray; set aside. Cook pasta according to package directions; drain. Return pasta to pan; set aside.

2 Meanwhile, in a large skillet heat oil over medium-high heat. Add mushrooms, onion, and garlic. Cook for 5 to 7 minutes or until mushrooms are tender, rich brown, and a little crisp around the edges, stirring frequently. Remove from heat. Stir in spinach.

3 Meanwhile, for the cheese sauce, in a medium saucepan melt butter over medium heat. Whisk in flour, nutmeg, and pepper. Cook and stir for 2 minutes. Whisk in milk. Cook and stir until thickened and bubbly. Reduce heat to low. Add 1 cup of the blue cheese; stir until cheese is melted.

4 Add cheese sauce and mushroom mixture to pasta; stir to combine. Spoon into the prepared baking dish. Sprinkle walnuts and remaining blue cheese over top.

5 Bake, uncovered, for 15 minutes or until heated through (160°F).

PER SERVING 415 **CAL**; 17 g **FAT** (7 g **SAT**); 25 mg **CHOL**; 313 mg **SODIUM**; 51 g **CARB**; 4 g **FIBER**; 16 g **PRO**

Sweet-Spicy Baked Beans

Salsa, steak seasoning, and a topping of crispy potato chips give this potluck favorite a few tasty twists.

MAKES 10 servings   **PREP** 15 minutes   **BAKE** 1 hour 45 minutes at 325°F

½   **cup packed brown sugar**
½   **cup ketchup**
¼   **cup bottled salsa**
¼   **cup bottled barbecue sauce**
¼   **cup yellow mustard or spicy brown mustard**
1½   **teaspoons steak seasoning**
1   **31-ounce can pork and beans in tomato sauce, undrained**
1   **16-ounce can butter beans, black beans, or pinto beans, rinsed and drained**
1   **16-ounce can dark red kidney beans, rinsed and drained**
½   **cup chopped onion (1 medium)**
    Potato chips, broken (optional)

1 Preheat oven to 325°F. In a large bowl stir together brown sugar, ketchup, salsa, barbecue sauce, mustard, and steak seasoning. Stir in pork and beans, butter beans, kidney beans, and onion. Transfer bean mixture to a lightly greased 2½- to 3-quart casserole.

2 Cover and bake for 1 hour. Uncover beans and stir. Bake, uncovered, for 45 minutes or until desired consistency, stirring occasionally. (Beans will thicken slightly as they cool.) If desired, top with broken potato chips.

PER SERVING 229 **CAL**; 1 g **FAT** (0 g **SAT**); 6 mg **CHOL**; 1,095 mg **SODIUM**; 47 g **CARB**; 8 g **FIBER**; 10 g **PRO**

Roasted Tomato Pasta with Mozzarella

With little balls of fresh mozzarella and a savory Mediterranean-style vinaigrette, this big-batch pasta salad is a welcome change of pace from the standard supermarket variety.

MAKES 12 servings   **PREP** 20 minutes   **ROAST** 20 minutes at 450°F   **STAND** 30 minutes

1	pound red and/or yellow grape or cherry tomatoes, halved
2	teaspoons dried oregano, crushed
3	cloves garlic, thinly sliced
1	teaspoon kosher salt
¼	cup olive oil
1	16-ounce package dried rotini pasta
⅓	cup olive oil
2	tablespoons white wine vinegar
½	teaspoon cracked black pepper
8	ounces small fresh mozzarella balls or cubed fresh mozzarella
½	cup snipped fresh basil

1 Preheat oven to 450°F. Arrange tomato halves, cut sides up, in a foil-lined 15×10×1-inch baking pan. Sprinkle with oregano, garlic, and salt; drizzle with the ¼ cup olive oil. Roast tomatoes, uncovered, for 20 to 25 minutes or until light brown and shriveled. Set aside.

2 Meanwhile, prepare pasta according to package directions; drain. In a large bowl whisk together the ⅓ cup olive oil, the vinegar, and pepper. Add warm pasta to bowl; toss to coat. Let cool to room temperature, stirring occasionally.

3 Add the tomatoes and any drippings from the pan, the mozzarella, and basil to the pasta. Toss to combine. Serve at room temperature.

PER SERVING 297 **CAL**; 15 g **FAT** (4 g **SAT**); 13 mg **CHOL**; 222 mg **SODIUM**; 30 g **CARB**; 2 g **FIBER**; 9 g **PRO**

Bacon Artichoke Potato Salad

Jan Laub claims that she is not a cook, like her twin sister is. The judges of the 2013 America's Best Potato Salad Challenge sponsored by Reser's Fine Foods might beg to differ. Jan, of Broken Arrow, Oklahoma, was one of 15 finalists Reser's invited to the World Food Championship in Las Vegas, where she won the contest and the $10,000 prize. To come up with this yummy potato salad recipe she asked herself what everyone likes to eat, and the answer was Hot Artichoke Dip. She started there and made the recipe. Her sister tried it, Jan tweaked it, then she sent it in. At the Championship, one of the Food Network celebrity judges told her it tasted like something his grandmother—who taught him to cook—would make. High praise, indeed.

MAKES 12 servings   **PREP** 25 minutes   **COOK** 15 minutes   **CHILL** 1 hour

2   **pounds small round red potatoes, quartered**
2   **tablespoons kosher or sea salt**
6   **slices bacon**
¾   **cup mayonnaise**
¾   **cup sour cream**
1   **teaspoon coarsely ground black pepper**
1   **teaspoon Dijon mustard**
1   **7.5-ounce jar marinated artichoke hearts, drained and coarsely chopped**
¾   **cup chopped red sweet pepper**
1   **4-ounce can diced green chiles**
2   **tablespoons chopped green onion (green top only)**

1 Place potatoes in a medium saucepan. Cover with cold water. Add 1 tablespoon of the salt. Bring to boiling. Reduce heat and simmer 15 to 20 minutes or just until fork tender.

2 Meanwhile, cook the bacon until crisp, reserving 2 tablespoons of the drippings. For the dressing, in a medium bowl combine reserved drippings, mayonnaise, sour cream, black pepper, and mustard. Stir in artichoke hearts, sweet pepper, chiles, green onion, and 2 to 3 teaspoons of the remaining salt, to taste.

3 While potatoes are still hot, add them to the dressing, tossing to coat. Chill 1 to 2 hours or until cold, stirring once or twice.

4 To serve, transfer to a serving dish, sprinkle with bacon.

PER SERVING 223 **CAL**; 17 g **FAT** (4 g **SAT**); 18 mg **CHOL**; 1,360 mg **SODIUM**; 14 g **CARB**; 2 g **FIBER**; 4 g **PRO**

Cheesy Mexican Potato Bake

This dish features the most appealing and popular potluck flavors and ingredients possible—cheese, potatoes, chiles, and Mexican spices—such as ground chile and cumin. It's a surefire hit!

MAKES 10 servings **PREP** 20 minutes **BAKE** 55 minutes at 350°F **STAND** 10 minutes

¾	**cup chopped red sweet pepper (1 medium)**
½	**cup chopped onion (1 medium)**
6	**tablespoons butter**
2	**tablespoons all-purpose flour**
2	**cups half-and-half or light cream**
12	**ounces process cheese food with jalapeños (such as Velveeta), cubed**
1	**teaspoon ground ancho chile pepper or chili powder**
½	**teaspoon ground cumin**
¼	**teaspoon black pepper**
1	**28-ounce package frozen diced hash brown potatoes with onions and peppers, thawed**
2	**cups tortilla chips, crushed if desired**
1	**to 2 fresh jalapeño peppers, sliced (see tip, page 54) (optional)**

1 Preheat oven to 350°F. Grease a 3-quart rectangular baking dish; set aside.

2 In a large skillet cook sweet pepper and onion in hot butter about 4 minutes or until tender. Stir in flour. Cook and stir for 1 minute. Stir in half-and-half and cheese. Stir until cheese is melted. Stir in ancho chile pepper, cumin, and black pepper. Stir in potatoes. Transfer to prepared baking dish. Cover with foil.

3 Bake for 45 minutes, stirring twice. Uncover and bake about 10 minutes more or until potatoes are tender when pierced with a fork and liquid is absorbed. Top with tortilla chips and, if desired, jalapeño slices.

PER SERVING 361 **CAL**; 23 g **FAT** (13 g **SAT**); 66 mg **CHOL**; 662 mg **SODIUM**; 30 g **CARB**; 3 g **FIBER**; 10 g **PRO**

Savory Double-Walnut Scones

Homemade breads are welcome at any type of gathering. These elegant quick breads are flavored with buttermilk, Dijon, honey, thyme, and tangy Gruyère cheese.

MAKES 16 servings   **PREP** 20 minutes   **BAKE** 7 minutes at 350°F/18 minutes at 375°F

1¼ **cups walnuts**
2¼ **cups all-purpose flour**
2   **teaspoons baking powder**
½   **teaspoon baking soda**
¼   **teaspoon salt**
½   **cup cold butter**
1   **cup Gruyère cheese, shredded (4 ounces)**
½   **teaspoon dried thyme, crushed, or 1½ teaspoons snipped fresh thyme**
1   **egg, lightly beaten**
1   **cup buttermilk**
1   **tablespoon honey**
1   **tablespoon Dijon mustard**
     Shredded Gruyère cheese, chopped walnuts, and snipped fresh thyme (optional)

1 Preheat oven to 350°F. Place 1¼ cups walnuts on a baking sheet. Bake for 7 to 9 minutes or until toasted. Coarsely chop 1 cup of the walnuts; set aside. Finely grind remaining walnuts; set aside. Increase oven temperature to 375°F.

2 In a large bowl combine flour, finely ground walnuts, baking powder, baking soda, and salt. Using a pastry blender, cut in butter until mixture resembles coarse meal. Stir in the 4 ounces Gruyère, 1 cup coarsely chopped walnuts, and thyme. Make a well in center of mixture. In a small bowl combine egg, buttermilk, honey, and mustard; add all at once to flour mixture. Using a fork, stir just until moistened.

3 Turn dough out onto a lightly floured surface. Knead dough by folding and gently pressing it for 10 to 12 strokes or until nearly smooth. Divide in half. Pat or lightly roll each half to a ¾-inch thick circle, about 6 inches in diameter. Cut each circle in eight triangles. Place triangles 2 inches apart on a greased baking sheets. Bake for 18 to 20 minutes or until golden brown.

4 Transfer to a cooling rack. If desired, top with additional cheese, walnuts, and thyme. Serve warm.

PER SERVING 220 **CAL**; 15 g **FAT** (6 g **SAT**); 37 mg **CHOL**; 229 mg **SODIUM**; 17 g **CARB**; 1 g **FIBER**; 6 g **PRO**

handheld favorites

Sandwiches, wraps, pizzas, and calzones tailor-made for casual eating.

MEXICAN PIZZA CON CHORIZO

BURGERS, SANDWICHES, AND WRAPS

Chicken Panini with Cilantro Mayonnaise, 152

Corned Beef and Cabbage Calzone, 150

Double Pork Cuban Sandwiches, 152

French-Toasted Sausage and Pear "Hot Dogs," 158

Lamb Kefta (Lebanese Lamb Kabobs), 148

Philadelphia Cheesesteak Wraps, 149

Raspberry Black Pepper Melt, 157

Sloppy Turkey and Chili Joes, 161

Sweet Skillet Meatball Banh Mi, 151

Turkey Reuben Loaf, 160

PIZZAS

Cauliflower-Crusted Pizza, 162

Mexican Pizza con Chorizo, 155

Lamb Kefta (Lebanese Lamb Kabobs)

By definition, "kefta" is the Moroccan word for ground meat. In practice, it's seasoned ground meat rolled into meatballs or wrapped around a skewer and grilled over a smoky fire. Kefta is one of Morocco's most popular street foods.

MAKES 4 servings   **PREP** 20 minutes   **GRILL** 10 minutes

2	**eggs, lightly beaten**
½	**cup soft bread crumbs**
⅓	**cup finely chopped onion**
4	**cloves garlic, minced**
2	**tablespoons snipped fresh parsley**
1	**tablespoon snipped fresh cilantro**
2	**teaspoons snipped fresh oregano**
2	**teaspoons snipped fresh mint**
½	**teaspoon salt**
½	**teaspoon ground cumin**
½	**teaspoon ground cinnamon**
¼	**teaspoon crushed red pepper (optional)**
1½	**pounds ground lamb**
4	**Greek pita flatbreads**
1	**recipe Cucumber-Yogurt Sauce**
	Lemon wedges (optional)
	Snipped fresh flat-leaf parsley, cilantro, oregano, and/or mint) (optional)

1 In a large bowl combine eggs, bread crumbs, onion, garlic, parsley, cilantro, oregano, mint, salt, cumin, cinnamon, and, if desired, crushed red pepper. Add lamb; mix well. Divide meat into four portions. Shape each portion into 4 meatballs. Thread meatballs on wooden (see tip, page 11) or metal skewers.

2 For a charcoal or gas grill, place kabobs on the grill rack directly over medium heat. Cover and grill for 10 to 12 minutes or until meatballs are done (160°F), turning once halfway through grilling.

3 Serve kabobs on flatbreads with Cucumber-Yogurt Sauce and, if desired, lemon wedges and additional fresh herbs.

Cucumber-Yogurt Sauce In a small bowl stir together ½ a small cucumber, seeded and finely chopped, and ¾ cup plain yogurt. Season to taste with salt and pepper.

PER SERVING 709 **CAL**; 37 g **FAT** (15 g **SAT**); 212 mg **CHOL**; 1,029 mg **SODIUM**; 51 g **CARB**; 3 g **FIBER**; 42 g **PRO**

Philadelphia Cheesesteak Wraps

This slow-cooker version of the traditional pepper-topped steak-and-cheese sandwich gets a slather of nose-tingling horseradish mayonnaise.

MAKES 6 servings   **PREP** 20 minutes   **SLOW COOK** 10 hours (low) or 5 hours (high)

- **1   pound beef flank steak**
- **1   tablespoon vegetable oil**
- **1   cup red sweet pepper strips (1 medium)**
- **1   cup thin onion wedges**
- **1½ teaspoons dried Italian seasoning, crushed**
- **1   14.5-ounce can beef broth**
- **½   cup mayonnaise**
- **4   teaspoons prepared horseradish**
- **6   10-inch flour tortillas**
- **3   slices provolone cheese, halved**

1 Trim fat from meat. In a large skillet cook meat in hot oil over medium-high heat until browned on both sides. Drain off fat. In a 4- to 5-quart slow cooker combine sweet pepper, onion, and Italian seasoning. Top with meat; pour broth over meat.

2 Cover and cook on low-heat setting for 10 to 12 hours or on high-heat setting for 5 to 6 hours.

3 Remove meat from cooker. Using two forks, pull meat apart into shreds. In a small bowl combine mayonnaise and horseradish; spread on one side of tortillas. Spoon shredded meat onto tortillas to one side of center. Using a slotted spoon, spoon sweet pepper and onion onto meat. Add cheese; roll up or fold tortilla over filling.

PER SERVING 484 **CAL**; 30 g **FAT** (8 g **SAT**); 48 mg **CHOL**; 627 mg **SODIUM**; 27 g **CARB**; 2 g **FIBER**; 25 g **PRO**

Corned Beef and Cabbage Calzone

With corned beef, cabbage, and Thousand Island dressing for dipping, this pocket sandwich takes the calzone out of the Italian sphere and places it directly in an American deli.

MAKES 4 servings   **PREP** 8 minutes   **COOK** 10 minutes   **BAKE** 12 minutes at 400°F

1	**teaspoon caraway seeds, lightly crushed**
6	**ounces cooked corned beef, finely chopped**
½	**medium red onion, thinly sliced**
1	**14- to 16-ounce package shredded cabbage with carrot (coleslaw mix)**
½	**teaspoon black pepper**
1	**13.8-ounce package refrigerated pizza dough**
	Bottled Thousand Island salad dressing (optional)

1 Preheat oven to 400°F. Lightly grease two baking sheets; set aside.

2 For filling, in an extra-large skillet lightly toast caraway seeds over medium-high heat. Add corned beef and onion. Cook and stir for 2 minutes. Add shredded cabbage with carrot and the pepper. Cook for 5 to 7 minutes or until cabbage is wilted. Remove from heat. Cover; set aside.

3 On a lightly floured surface, unroll pizza dough. Roll dough into a 16-inch square. Cut into quarters with a pizza cutter or kitchen shears. If necessary, drain filling to remove excess liquid. Place one-fourth of the filling on each dough piece. Moisten edges with water and fold dough over filling to form a rectangle. Roll up edges. Press edges with a fork to seal. Place on the prepared baking sheets.

4 Bake for 12 to 14 minutes or until golden brown, rotating sheets halfway through baking time. Using a large metal spatula, transfer calzones to a wire rack. Cool for 1 minute. If desired, serve with Thousand Island dressing.

PER SERVING 380 **CAL**; 11 g **FAT** (3 g **SAT**); 42 mg **CHOL**; 1,206 mg **SODIUM**; 54 g **CARB**; 4 g **FIBER**; 17 g **PRO**

Sweet Skillet Meatball Banh Mi

Banh mi are a product of the nearly century-long French colonization of Vietnam, which ended in the mid 1950s. Crisp French rolls are filled with seasoned meat (most often pork) and topped with vegetables, herbs, and chiles. This twist features beef meatballs cooked in a sweetened soy sauce glaze.

MAKES 6 servings **START TO FINISH** 40 minutes

1 egg, lightly beaten
¼ cup fine dry bread crumbs
3 tablespoons soy sauce
1 clove garlic, minced
1 pound ground beef
3 medium carrots, cut into thin bite-size strips
1 medium onion, thinly sliced
2 tablespoons packed brown sugar
1 9-ounce package fresh spinach
6 hoagie buns, split and toasted
   Fresh flat-leaf parsley leaves (optional)

1 In a large bowl combine egg, bread crumbs, 1 tablespoon of the soy sauce, and the garlic. Add ground beef; mix well. Shape into 1¼-inch meatballs. (You should get about 30 meatballs.)

2 In an extra-large heavy skillet arrange meatballs in a single layer. Cook over medium-high heat for 8 to 10 minutes or until browned on all sides, turning to brown evenly. Remove from skillet; keep warm.

3 Add carrots and onion to skillet. Cook and stir for 3 to 5 minutes or until tender.

4 Return meatballs to skillet. Add brown sugar and the remaining 2 tablespoons soy sauce. Cook about 2 minutes more or until meatballs and vegetables are well coated. Add spinach; cook about 3 minutes or just until spinach is wilted. Divide vegetable-meatball mixture among hoagie buns. If desired, sprinkle with parsley.

PER SERVING 445 **CAL**; 15 g **FAT** (5 g **SAT**); 82 mg **CHOL**; 1,066 mg **SODIUM**; 55 g **CARB**; 4 g **FIBER**; 24 g **PRO**

Chicken Panini with Cilantro Mayonnaise

Be sure to remove the skin from the chicken before cooking it. Chicken crisps in the oven, it steams in a slow cooker.

MAKES 6 servings   **PREP** 30 minutes   **SLOW COOK** 6 hours (low) or 3 hours (high)   **GRILL** 2 minutes

2	cloves garlic, minced
¼	teaspoon salt
¼	teaspoon black pepper
2	pounds bone-in chicken breast halves, skinned
½	cup water
12	½-inch slices whole grain Italian or French bread
1	recipe Cilantro Mayonnaise
6	¼-inch slices fresh pineapple, quartered
2	cups lightly packed fresh baby spinach leaves Nonstick cooking spray

1 Sprinkle garlic, salt, and pepper evenly over chicken, rubbing in with fingers. Place chicken in a 3½- or 4-quart slow cooker. Add ½ cup water.

2 Cover and cook on low-heat for 6 to 6½ hours or on high-heat for 3 to 3¼ hours. Remove chicken from cooker. Let stand until cool enough to handle. Remove and discard chicken bones. Using two forks, coarsely shred chicken.

3 Spread half the bread with Cilantro Mayonnaise. Layer chicken, pineapple, spinach, and remaining bread. Coat both sides of sandwiches with cooking spray.

4 Lightly coat an unheated panini griddle or large nonstick skillet with cooking spray. Heat griddle according to manufacturer's directions, or preheat skillet over medium heat. For griddle, close lid and cook 2 to 3 minutes or until toasted. For skillet, place a heavy plate on sandwiches. Cook 1 to 2 minutes or until bottoms are toasted. Carefully remove hot plate. Turn sandwiches and top with plate. Cook 1 to 2 minutes or until toasted. Cut sandwiches in half to serve.

Cilantro Mayonnaise In a small bowl combine ⅓ cup light mayonnaise, ¼ cup snipped fresh cilantro, 2 tablespoons honey mustard, and ½ teaspoon finely shredded lime peel.

PER SERVING 331 **CAL**; 8 g **FAT** (1 g **SAT**); 68 mg **CHOL**; 504 mg **SODIUM**; 32 g **CARB**; 3 g **FIBER**; 29 g **PRO**

Double Pork Cuban Sandwiches

The Cuban—hot ham and cheese layered with pickles, mustard, Swiss cheese, and sometimes roasted pork or bacon—got its name from immigrant Cuban workers in Key West, Tampa, and Miami in the mid-19th century.

MAKES 4 servings   **START TO FINISH** 30 minutes

2	tablespoons Dijon mustard
2	tablespoons mayonnaise or salad dressing
1	teaspoon lime juice
⅛	teaspoon ground cumin
4	English muffins or ciabatta buns, split
8	ounces thinly sliced cooked ham
8	slices packaged ready-to-serve cooked bacon
8	lengthwise sandwich pickle slices
4	slices provolone or Swiss cheese (about 4 ounces)
1	tablespoon butter, softened

1 In a small bowl combine mustard, mayonnaise, lime juice, and cumin. Spread cut sides of muffin halves with mayonnaise mixture. Place ham on bottoms of muffin halves. Layer with bacon and pickle slices; top with cheese. Place tops of muffin halves, spread sides down, on sandwiches. Spread outsides of sandwiches with butter.

2 Preheat a covered indoor grill, panini press, grill pan, or large skillet. Place sandwiches, half at a time if necessary, in grill or panini press. Cover and cook for 6 to 8 minutes or until golden brown and cheese is melted. (If using a grill pan or skillet, place sandwiches on grill pan or skillet. Weight sandwiches down with a heavy skillet [add food cans for more weight] and cook for 2 minutes. Turn sandwiches over, weight down, and cook for 2 to 3 minutes more or until golden brown and cheese is melted.)

PER SERVING 426 **CAL**; 22 g **FAT** (10 g **SAT**); 65 mg **CHOL**; 1,755 mg **SODIUM**; 29 g **CARB**; 2 g **FIBER**; 24 g **PRO**

Mexican Pizza con Chorizo

Baking the topped tortillas on a hot baking stone gives them a crisp, flaky crust.

MAKES 8 servings   **PREP** 20 minutes   **BAKE** 4 minutes at 450°F

1	teaspoon olive oil
½	cup chopped onion (1 medium)
6	cloves garlic, minced
	Pinch salt
2	teaspoons chili powder
1	teaspoon ground cumin
1	15.5-ounce can black beans, undrained
3	to 4 tablespoons water
4	12-inch flour tortillas
2	cups shredded Oaxaca or Monterey Jack cheese (8 ounces)
4	ounces cooked smoked chorizo, thinly sliced
2	cups mesclun or shredded cabbage
1	cup salsa
½	cup snipped fresh cilantro
1	fresh jalapeño, stemmed, seeded, and thinly sliced (see tip, page 54) (optional)

1 Place a pizza stone on the bottom rack of the oven. Preheat oven to 450°F.

2 In a small saucepan heat oil over medium-high heat. Add onion, garlic, and salt; cook for 3 minutes or until onion and garlic are tender. Stir in chili powder and cumin; cook for 1 minute more. Remove from heat; stir in beans and 3 tablespoons of the water. Transfer mixture to a food processor or blender. Pulse until bean mixture is spreadable but still chunky, adding more water if necessary.

3 One tortilla at a time, evenly spread a thin layer of the bean mixture on tortilla. Top with ½ cup of the cheese and one-fourth of the chorizo. Transfer topped tortilla to the pizza stone. Bake for 4 to 5 minutes or until cheese is bubbly and edges are crisp.

4 Transfer tortillas to a cutting board; cool for 1 minute. Top each pizza with ½ cup of the mesclun, ¼ cup of the salsa, 2 tablespoons of the cilantro, and, if desired, a few chile pepper slices. Cut each pizza into wedges before serving.

PER SERVING 348 **CAL**; 16 g **FAT** (3 g **SAT**); 37 mg **CHOL**; 912 mg **SODIUM**; 36 g **CARB**; 6 g **FIBER**; 18 g **PRO**

Raspberry Black Pepper Melt

Given the simplicity of the base ingredients of grilled cheese sandwiches—cheese and bread— the array of flavor combinations is almost infinite. When Kelly Aldrich of Spokane, Washington, made these toasty sandwiches at work (which happens to be her church), her co-workers loved them. They were also a hit with the judges of the 2014 Tillamook Cheese Factory Grilled Cheese Contest. The winning combination of Tillamook® smoked black pepper white cheddar cheese and raspberry jam earned her $500 and a gift basket of Tillamook goodies.

MAKES 4 servings **PREP** 15 minutes **COOK** 4 minutes

- **8 slices soft white bread**
- **6 tablespoons Tillamook® unsalted butter, softened**
- **6 tablespoons raspberry jam with seeds**
- **4 ounces Tillamook® smoked black pepper white cheddar cheese, sliced into 16 slices**
- **⅔ cup finely diced cooked chicken (4 ounces)**

1 Place bread slices on a work surface. Spread butter on one side of each slice of bread. Turn slices over. Spread jam on each slice of bread. Arrange 4 cheese slices on each of 4 slices of the bread. Top cheese with chicken. Top with remaining bread slices, jam sides down (use a wide spatula to lift bread from work surface, if necessary).

2 Heat an extra-large skillet over medium heat, or heat an electric griddle to 275°F. Place the sandwiches in the skillet and grill for 2 to 3 minutes per side or until golden brown and cheese is melted. Cut each sandwich in half diagonally.

PER SERVING 537 **CAL**; 30 g **FAT** (18 g **SAT**); 101 mg **CHOL**; 458 mg **SODIUM**; 46 g **CARB**; 2 g **FIBER**; 20 g **PRO**

French-Toasted Sausage and Pear "Hot Dogs"

The humble hot dog takes an elegant turn. These sandwiches feature applewood-smoked chicken sausage, pears, and provolone tucked into hot dog buns given a French toast treatment. The buns are dipped in a mixture of eggs, half-and-half, sugar, vanilla, cinnamon, and nutmeg—then cooked in hot butter.

MAKES 6 servings   **PREP** 25 minutes   **COOK** 6 minutes

12	ounces fully cooked applewood smoked chicken sausage links
1	tablespoon vegetable oil
2	eggs
½	cup half-and-half or light cream
1	tablespoon sugar
1	teaspoon vanilla
⅛	teaspoon ground cinnamon
⅛	teaspoon ground nutmeg
6	Hawaiian sweet hot dog buns or regular frankfurter buns, split
2	tablespoons honey (if using regular hot dog buns)
6	thin slices provolone cheese
½	medium red pear, cored and thinly sliced
1	to 2 tablespoons butter or vegetable oil
	Maple syrup

1 Cut chicken sausage lengthwise into ¼- to ½-inch-thick slices. In a large skillet heat 1 tablespoon oil over medium-high heat. Brown sliced chicken sausage on both sides. Drain on paper towels. Wipe out skillet with paper towels; set aside.

2 Meanwhile, in a shallow dish whisk together eggs, half-and-half, sugar, vanilla, cinnamon, and nutmeg; set aside.

3 Drizzle cut sides of buns with honey. Add a slice of cheese to each bun. Fill with sliced chicken sausage and pear. Secure buns with wooden toothpicks.

4 In the large skillet heat butter over medium heat. Dip 3 filled buns in egg mixture; add to skillet. Cook until well browned, about 3 to 4 minutes per side*. Repeat with remaining filled buns. Remove toothpicks. Serve with maple syrup.

*Keep French toast warm in a rectangular baking dish in a 200°F oven.

PER SERVING 551 **CAL**; 23 g **FAT** (12 g **SAT**); 159 mg **CHOL**; 734 mg **SODIUM**; 63 g **CARB**; 1 g **FIBER**; 23 g **PRO**

Turkey Reuben Loaf

When a Reuben sandwich is made with turkey and coleslaw instead of corned beef and sauerkraut, it's often called a Rachel. This sandwich roll—which leans toward the Rachel—features a quick homemade Russian dressing.

MAKES 4 servings   **PREP** 15 minutes   **BAKE** 12 minutes at 400°F

½	**cup mayonnaise**
¼	**cup pickle relish**
1	**tablespoon ketchup**
2	**cups shredded cabbage**
2	**teaspoons vinegar**
1	**teaspoon caraway seeds**
½	**unsliced oblong loaf bread**
6	**ounces Havarti cheese, sliced**
8	**ounces cooked turkey, sliced or chopped**

1 Preheat oven to 400°F. For sauce, in a small bowl combine mayonnaise, pickle relish, and ketchup; set aside sauce. In a medium bowl combine cabbage, vinegar, and caraway seeds; set aside cabbage mixture.

2 Slice bread lengthwise. Hollow out and remove some of the bread for sandwich fillings. Spread some of the sauce over cut sides of bread. Arrange half the cheese slices on bottom half of bread. Top with cabbage mixture, turkey, and the remaining cheese. Top with top half of bread. Wrap tightly in foil; place on a baking sheet.

3 Bake for 10 minutes. Carefully unwrap and bake for 2 to 3 minutes more or until bread is crisp and cheese is melted.

4 To serve, using a serrated knife, cut loaf into slices. Pass the remaining sauce.

PER SERVING 640 **CAL**; 40 g **FAT** (13 g **SAT**); 85 mg **CHOL**; 931 mg **SODIUM**; 37 g **CARB**; 5 g **FIBER**; 31 g **PRO**

Sloppy Turkey and Chili Joes

A quick barbecue sauce spiked with chili powder gives these Sloppy Joes a hint of Tex-Mex taste.

MAKES 4 servings   **START TO FINISH** 35 minutes

1   to 1¼ pounds ground turkey breast
½   cup chopped onion (1 medium)
1   medium fresh poblano chile pepper, seeded and chopped (see tip, page 54)
1   15-ounce can tomato sauce
2   tablespoons packed brown sugar
1   tablespoon Worcestershire sauce
2   teaspoons chili powder
½   teaspoon garlic powder
    Salt
    Black pepper
4   kaiser rolls, split and toasted
    Fresh basil leaves (optional)
4   slices Monterey Jack cheese
    Green and/or red sweet pepper rings (optional)
    Thinly sliced tomato (optional)
    Thinly sliced onion (optional)

1 In a large nonstick skillet cook ground turkey, onion, and chile pepper over medium heat until turkey is no longer pink, using a wooden spoon to break up turkey as it cooks. Stir in tomato sauce, brown sugar, Worcestershire sauce, chili powder, and garlic powder. Bring to boiling; reduce heat. Simmer, covered, for 15 minutes, stirring occasionally. Season to taste with salt and black pepper.

2 Place bottoms of rolls on individual plates; if desired, top with basil leaves. Add cheese slices. Top with turkey chili and, if desired, sweet pepper, tomato, and/or onion. Replace tops of rolls.

PER SERVING 470 **CAL**; 10 g **FAT** (5 g **SAT**); 84 mg **CHOL**; 1,119 mg **SODIUM**; 53 g **CARB**; 3 g **FIBER**; 41 g **PRO**

Cauliflower-Crusted Pizza

Cutting carbs? This innovative pie has a foundation made of cauliflower blended with egg, bread crumbs, seasoning, and cheese. In Step 2 squeeze as much liquid out of the cauliflower as possible to ensure the crispiest crust.

MAKES 4 servings   **PREP** 30 minutes   **MICROWAVE** 3 minutes   **BAKE** 17 minutes at 425°F

1   **medium head cauliflower (1½ to 2 pounds), cored and cut into florets (4 cups)**
2   **tablespoons water**
1   **egg, lightly beaten**
¼   **cup shredded Italian cheese blend (1 ounce)**
¼   **cup grated Parmesan cheese**
¼   **cup panko bread crumbs**
½   **teaspoon Italian seasoning, crushed**
¼   **teaspoon salt**
2   **cups sliced fresh mushrooms**
1   **cup yellow or green sweet pepper strips**
1   **small red onion, cut into thin wedges**
1   **teaspoon olive oil**
¾   **cup pizza sauce**
½   **to ¾ cup shredded Italian cheese blend**
     Fresh oregano, basil, and/or parsley leaves

1 Place the cauliflower in a food processor. Cover and pulse four to six times or until crumbly and resembles the texture of couscous.

2 Place a pizza stone or baking sheet in the oven. Preheat oven to 425°F. Place cauliflower in a microwave-safe casserole with 2 tablespoons water. Microwave, covered, on high for 3 to 4 minutes or until tender, stirring once or twice. Cool. Transfer cauliflower to a 100% cotton flour-sack towel. Wrap towel around cauliflower and squeeze until there is no more liquid (this step is critical).

3 In a medium bowl stir together cooked and drained cauliflower, egg, the ¼ cup Italian cheese blend, the Parmesan cheese, panko, Italian seasoning, and salt. On a piece of parchment paper pat cauliflower mixture into a 12-inch circle. Transfer crust on paper to the preheated pizza stone. Bake for 12 to 15 minutes or until crisp and starting to brown.

4 Meanwhile, in a large skillet cook and stir mushrooms, sweet pepper, and onion in hot oil for 4 to 6 minutes or until crisp-tender. Remove from heat.

5 Spoon pizza sauce over baked crust, spreading evenly. Top with cooked vegetables. Sprinkle evenly with the ½ cup Italian cheese blend. Bake for 5 minutes more or until heated through and cheese is melted. If desired, sprinkle with snipped fresh herb(s). Cut into slices to serve.

PER SERVING 264 **CAL**; 14 g **FAT** (7 g **SAT**); 76 mg **CHOL**; 773 mg **SODIUM**; 18 g **CARB**; 4 g **FIBER**; 17 g **PRO**

CHAPTER 9
sweet
endings

Save the best for last—cakes, cookies, bars, brownies, pies, and puddings.

SALTED CHOCOLATE-
CARAMEL ROUNDS

Rhubarb and Strawberry Coffee Cake

Nestled in the heart of Pennsylvania Dutch Country, Kitchen Kettle Village—a collection of quaint shops, restaurants and hotels—sponsors a rhubarb dessert contest during its annual Rhubarb Festival. In 2014, Lynne Dohne of Lancaster, Pennsylvania, picked up the top prize for this gooey coffee cake. Kitchen Kettle Village designates part of its proceeds each year to a good cause. This year it was farm preservation. Lynn donated a portion of the $250 prize money to that cause and used the rest on a trip to Disney World with her granddaughter.

MAKES 12 servings   **PREP** 30 minutes   **BAKE** 35 minutes at 350°F

1	package 2-layer-size yellow cake mix
½	cup packed brown sugar
2	tablespoons butter
⅔	cup chopped pecans
1	8-ounce carton sour cream
2	eggs
¼	cup all-purpose flour
1½	cups finely chopped fresh rhubarb
1½	cups sliced fresh strawberries
½	cup butter
¾	cup granulated sugar
½	cup evaporated milk
½	teaspoon vanilla

1 Preheat oven to 350°F. Grease a 13×9×2-inch baking pan; set aside. For the streusel, in a small bowl combine ½ cup of the cake mix and the brown sugar. Using a pastry blender cut 2 tablespoons butter into mixture until it resembles coarse crumbs. Stir in nuts; set aside.

2 For the cake, in a large bowl combine sour cream, eggs, flour, and remaining cake mix. Beat with mixer on low for 30 seconds. Beat on medium for 2 minutes more. Fold in rhubarb and strawberries. Spread batter in prepared pan. Sprinkle streusel over the batter.

3 Bake for 35 to 40 minutes or until a toothpick inserted near the center comes out clean. Cool completely on a wire rack.

4 For the vanilla glaze, in a small saucepan melt ½ cup butter over medium heat. Stir in granulated sugar and evaporated milk. Bring to boiling; reduce heat and simmer, uncovered, for 3 to 5 minutes or until slightly thickened. Remove from heat, stir in vanilla. Drizzle over cooled cake.

PER SERVING 480 **CAL**; 24 g **FAT** (10 g **SAT**); 70 mg **CHOL**; 413 mg **SODIUM**; 62 g **CARB**; 2 g **FIBER**; 5 g **PRO**

Butterscotch Marble Cake

Swirls of butterscotch and chocolate catch the eye in this simple but impressive dessert that starts with a cake mix and a package of instant pudding.

MAKES 12 servings   **PREP** 20 minutes   **BAKE** 55 minutes at 350°F   **COOL** 2 hours

- **1**   **package 2-layer-size white cake mix**
- **1**   **4-serving-size package butterscotch instant pudding and pie filling mix**
- **1**   **cup water**
- **4**   **eggs**
- **¼**   **cup vegetable oil**
- **½**   **cup chocolate-flavor syrup**
- **2**   **ounces sweet baking chocolate, chopped**
- **2**   **tablespoons butter**
- **¾**   **cup powdered sugar**
- **1**   **tablespoon hot water**

1 Preheat oven to 350°F. Grease and flour a 10-inch fluted tube pan; set aside.

2 In a large mixing bowl combine cake mix, pudding mix, the 1 cup water, the eggs, and oil. Beat with a mixer on low just until combined. Beat on medium for 2 minutes, scraping sides of bowl occasionally.

3 Transfer 1½ cups of the batter to a medium bowl; stir in chocolate syrup. Pour light-color batter into the prepared pan. Top with the chocolate batter. Using a table knife or thin metal spatula, gently cut through batters to swirl.

4 Bake for 55 to 60 minutes or until a wooden toothpick inserted near the center comes out clean. Cool in pan on a wire rack for 15 minutes. Remove cake from pan; cool completely on wire rack.

5 For icing, in a small saucepan combine sweet baking chocolate and the butter. Stir over low heat until melted. Remove from heat. Stir in powdered sugar and the 1 tablespoon hot water. If necessary, stir in additional hot water, 1 teaspoon at a time, until icing reaches drizzling consistency. Drizzle icing over cooled cake.

PER SERVING 377 **CAL**; 14 g **FAT** (4 g **SAT**); 76 mg **CHOL**; 467 mg **SODIUM**; 60 g **CARB**; 1 g **FIBER**; 5 g **PRO**

Spiced Sugar Cream Pie

Ground pecans, flour, and butter are combined in a delicate crust for this custardy pie. Nutmeg, cinnamon, and cloves infuse the traditional cream pie filling with warm flavor.

MAKES 8 servings   **PREP** 25 minutes   **BAKE** 50 minutes at 350°F   **CHILL** 2 hours

¾   **cup packed brown sugar**
⅓   **cup all-purpose flour**
¼   **cup granulated sugar**
½   **teaspoon freshly grated nutmeg or ¼ teaspoon ground nutmeg**
½   **teaspoon ground cinnamon**
     Dash ground cloves (optional)
2½ **cups whipping cream**
1   **vanilla bean, split lengthwise, or 1 teaspoon vanilla**
1   **recipe Nut Pastry Shell**
1   **recipe Sugar Sprinkle (optional)**

1 Preheat oven to 350°F. For filling, in a large bowl combine brown sugar, flour, granulated sugar, nutmeg, cinnamon, and, if desired, cloves, breaking up clumps of brown sugar. Slowly whisk cream into sugar mixture. If using, scrape seeds from vanilla bean. Whisk vanilla bean seeds or vanilla into sugar mixture.

2 Pour filling into Nut Pastry Shell. To prevent overbrowning, cover edge of pie with foil.

3 Place pie on middle oven rack. Bake for 25 minutes; remove foil. Bake for 25 to 30 minutes more or until top is lightly browned and filling is bubbly across the surface (pie won't appear set but will firm up upon cooling). Cool completely on a wire rack.

4 Cover; chill within 2 hours. Chill for 2 to 24 hours or until set. If desired, just before serving, cut pie and use a fine-mesh sieve to sift Sugar Sprinkle over pie.

Nut Pastry Shell In a medium bowl stir together 1¼ cups all-purpose flour, ¼ cup finely ground pecans, and ½ teaspoon salt. Using a pastry blender, cut in ¼ cup shortening and ¼ cup butter until pieces are pea size. Sprinkle 1 tablespoon ice water over part of the flour mixture; toss gently with a fork. Push moistened dough to side of bowl. Repeat with additional ice water, 1 tablespoon at a time (¼ to ⅓ cup total), until all the flour mixture is moistened. Gather pastry into a ball, kneading gently until it holds together. On a lightly floured surface, use your hands to slightly flatten pastry. Roll pastry from center to

edge into a 12-inch circle. Wrap around rolling pin; unroll into a 9-inch pie plate. Ease pastry into pie plate without stretching it. Trim pastry to ½ inch beyond edge of pie plate. Fold under extra pastry even with edge of plate. Crimp edge as desired. Do not prick pastry.

Sugar Sprinkle In a small bowl combine 1 tablespoon powdered sugar, a dash of ground nutmeg, and a dash of cinnamon.

PER SERVING 584 **CAL**; 42 g **FAT** (23 g **SAT**); 118 mg **CHOL**; 221 mg **SODIUM**; 48 g **CARB**; 1 g **FIBER**; 5 g **PRO**

Chocolate-Peanut Butter Cheesecake

For fans of PB&C, it doesn't get much better than this indulgent cheesecake. Layers of peanut butter and chocolate filling cover a crust made from crushed peanut butter-stuffed sandwich cookies.

MAKES 12 servings   **PREP** 35 minutes   **STAND** 30 minutes   **BAKE** 53 minutes at 350°F   **COOL** 2 hours   **CHILL** 4 hours

3   **8-ounce packages cream cheese**
3   **eggs**
2   **cups finely crushed peanut butter-filled peanut sandwich cookies**
¼   **cup butter, melted**
12 **ounces semisweet chocolate, chopped**
1   **cup whipping cream**
½   **cup creamy peanut butter**
1¼ **cups packed brown sugar**
2   **teaspoons vanilla**
15 **miniature chocolate-covered peanut butter cups, halved or coarsely chopped**

1 Allow cream cheese and eggs to stand at room temperature for 30 minutes. Meanwhile, preheat oven to 350°F. For crust, in a medium bowl combine crushed cookies and melted butter. Press mixture onto the bottom and 1½ inches up the sides of a 9-inch springform pan. Bake for 8 minutes. Cool on a wire rack.

2 For the chocolate layer, in a small saucepan combine chocolate and whipping cream. Stir frequently over low heat until chocolate is melted and mixture is smooth. Pour 1½ cups of the chocolate mixture into crust-lined pan, spreading evenly. Chill in the freezer for 10 minutes.

3 For the peanut butter layer, in a large mixing bowl beat cream cheese and peanut butter with a mixer on medium to high until smooth. Beat in brown sugar until combined. Using a fork, lightly beat eggs. Add eggs to cream cheese mixture, beating just until combined. Stir in vanilla. Pour cream cheese filling over chocolate layer in pan.

4 Bake for 45 minutes or until a 2½-inch area around edge appears set when gently shaken. Cool in pan on a wire rack for 15 minutes. Using a small sharp knife, loosen crust from sides of pan. Cool for 30 minutes more. Remove sides of pan. Cool cheesecake completely on wire rack. Spread the remaining chocolate mixture over top of cheesecake. Top with peanut butter cups. Cover and chill for at least 4 hours or overnight before serving.

PER SERVING 746 **CAL**; 53 g **FAT** (27 g **SAT**); 146 mg **CHOL**; 397 mg **SODIUM**; 64 g **CARB**; 3 g **FIBER**; 12 g **PRO**

Almighty Apple Pie

If a book were written about John Sunvold, it might be called The Professor and His Pies. *The Winter Springs, Florida, resident teaches speech at Seminole State College and political science at Valencia College. When he's not in the lecture hall, he's in the kitchen perfecting his pie-baking skills. John has entered the American Pie Council National Championships for 7 years and won the National Pie Championship 3 of those years. This pie—which featured four apple varieties and a lard crust—took top honors in the apple division. John won $200 and bragging rights.*

MAKES 8 servings   **PREP** 45 minutes   **CHILL** overnight + 3 hours   **COOK** 5 minutes   **BAKE** 1 hour 5 minutes at 350°F

2¼ cups King Arthur® unbleached all-purpose flour
1   tablespoon granulated sugar
½   teaspoon salt
½   cup unsalted butter, chilled
½   cup lard, chilled
⅓   cup cold water
30 Kraft® caramels, unwrapped
¼   cup milk
¾   cup pecan pieces
6   ounces cream cheese, softened
⅓   cup powdered sugar
6   ounces Cool Whip® Whipped Topping, thawed
7 to 8 cups coarsely peeled and chopped apples
1   cup packed brown sugar
¼   cup butter, melted
¼   cup apple juice concentrate
3   tablespoons cornstarch
1 to 2 teaspoons ground cinnamon
    Whipped cream or Cool Whip®, caramel sauce, and/or chopped pecans (optional)

1 For the crust, in a food processor place flour, granulated sugar, and salt. Pulse to combine. Add cold butter and lard; pulse until pieces resemble coarse crumbs.

2 Drizzle the cold water, about 1 tablespoon at a time, through feed tube while pulsing just until pastry begins to come together (do not overprocess). Gather pastry into a ball and shape into a disk; wrap disk in plastic wrap and chill overnight.

3 Preheat oven to 350°F. On a lightly floured surface roll pastry into a 13-inch circle. Ease pastry into a 9- or 10-inch pie plate*. Trim pastry to ½ inch beyond edge of pie plate (you may have more pastry than you need). Fold under extra crust and crimp as desired. Prick bottom and sides of pastry with a fork. Line crust with a double layer of foil. Bake for 30 minutes. Remove foil and bake for 5 minutes more or until set and dry. Remove from oven and cool completely on a wire rack.

4 For the caramel layer, in a small saucepan combine caramels and milk. Stir constantly over medium heat until melted and smooth. Reserve one-third of the melted caramel; set aside. Add pecans to caramel in saucepan; stir to combine. Spread caramel-pecan mixture over cooled crust. Chill 1 hour or until set.

5 For the cream layer, in a medium bowl combine cream cheese and powdered sugar. Fold in the 6 ounces thawed Cool Whip. Evenly spread over caramel layer. Drizzle with the reserved caramel; gently swirl into the cream layer. Chill for 1 hour.

6 Meanwhile, preheat oven to 350°F. For the apple layer, in an extra-large bowl combine apples, brown sugar, ¼ cup melted butter, apple juice concentrate, cornstarch, and cinnamon. Transfer apples to a 3-quart baking dish; cover with foil. Bake for 30 to 35 minutes or until apples are tender, stirring occasionally. Refrigerate for 1 hour or until fully chilled, stirring occasionally.

7 Spoon chilled apples onto cream layer. Serve immediately or chill up to 24 hours. If desired, top with whipped cream or additional Cool Whip, caramel sauce, and/or pecans.

* Or a 10-inch deep-dish pie plate.

PER SERVING 959 **CAL**; 53 g **FAT** (28 g **SAT**); 82 mg **CHOL**; 371 mg **SODIUM**; 113 g **CARB**; 4 g **FIBER**; 8 g **PRO**

Blueberry Crumble Slab Pie

When you need a big dessert for a big crowd, make a slab pie. This juicy, crumb-topped blueberry pie makes 24 servings. Serve it warm with vanilla ice cream.

MAKES 24 servings   **PREP** 30 minutes   **BAKE** 40 minutes at 375°F

2½   **cups all-purpose flour**
¾   **teaspoon salt**
¾   **cup butter-flavor shortening**
8   **to 10 tablespoons ice water**
1   **cup granulated sugar**
¼   **cup all-purpose flour**
½   **teaspoon ground cinnamon**
½   **teaspoon finely shredded lemon peel**
6   **cups fresh or frozen blueberries***
1   **recipe Crumb Topping**

1 Preheat oven to 375°F. For pastry, in a large bowl stir together the 2½ cups flour and the salt. Using a pastry blender, cut in shortening until pieces are pea size. Sprinkle 1 tablespoon of the ice water over part of the flour mixture; toss gently with a fork. Push moistened pastry to side of bowl. Repeat moistening flour mixture, using 1 tablespoon of the ice water at a time, until all of the flour mixture is moistened. Gather pastry into a ball, kneading gently until it holds together.

2 On a lightly floured surface, roll pastry into a 19×13-inch rectangle. Wrap pastry around the rolling pin; unroll into a 15×10×1-inch baking pan. Ease pastry onto the bottom and up the sides without stretching it. Trim pastry to ½ inch beyond edges of pan. Fold under extra pastry and crimp edges as desired.

3 In a large bowl stir together sugar, ¼ cup flour, the cinnamon, and lemon peel. Add blueberries; toss gently to coat. Spoon blueberry filling evenly into pastry-lined baking pan. Sprinkle with Crumb Topping.

4 Bake for 40 to 45 minutes or until filling is bubbly and topping is golden. If necessary to prevent overbrowning, cover top of pie loosely with foil for the last 10 minutes of baking. Cool slightly in pan on a wire rack. Serve warm or cool completely. Cut into bars.

Crumb Topping In a large bowl stir together 1 cup rolled oats, 1 cup packed brown sugar, and ½ cup all-purpose flour. Using a pastry blender, cut in ½ cup butter until oat mixture resembles coarse crumbs. Stir in ½ cup chopped pecans.

***Tip** If using frozen blueberries, toss with the sugar mixture as directed, then let stand at room temperature for 30 minutes before adding to the pastry-lined pan. Berries will still be icy.

PER SERVING 267 **CAL**; 12 g **FAT** (4 g **SAT**); 10 mg **CHOL**; 103 mg **SODIUM**; 38 g **CARB**; 2 g **FIBER**; 3 g **PRO**

Ginger Pear Galette

As elegant as it looks, this French-style pastry is actually simple to make. The edges are built up using layers of strips cut from thawed puff pastry.

MAKES 9 servings   **PREP** 25 minutes   **BAKE** 25 minutes at 400°F

½   **17.3-ounce package (1 sheet) frozen puff pastry sheets, thawed**
1   **egg white, lightly beaten**
2   **tablespoons all-purpose flour**
2   **tablespoons granulated sugar**
2   **tablespoons packed brown sugar**
1   **tablespoon finely chopped crystallized ginger**
1   **teaspoon finely shredded lemon peel**
2   **tablespoons butter**
3   **large pears, peeled and thinly sliced**
    Whipped cream (optional)

1 Preheat oven to 400°F. Line a baking sheet with parchment paper; set aside. On a lightly floured surface, unfold pastry. Roll into a 14×11-inch rectangle; trim to a 12×10-inch rectangle. Place on the prepared baking sheet. Brush edges of pastry with egg white. Cut ½-inch strips from pastry trimmings. Place strips on edges of pastry rectangle, pressing to form raised rim; trim ends. Brush edges again with egg white. If desired, decorate edges with cutouts from pastry trimmings and brush cutouts with egg white. Prick center of pastry rectangle with a fork.

2 For topping, in a small bowl stir together flour, granulated sugar, brown sugar, crystallized ginger, and lemon peel. Cut in butter until pieces are pea size.

3 Sprinkle half the topping over pastry. Arrange pear slices on tart, overlapping slightly. Sprinkle with remaining topping.

4 Bake for 25 minutes or until pastry is golden and pears are tender. If desired, top with whipped cream. Serve warm.

PER SERVING 282 **CAL**; 15 g **FAT** (5 g **SAT**); 8 mg **CHOL**; 106 mg **SODIUM**; 36 g **CARB**; 3 g **FIBER**; 3 g **PRO**

Blackberry Cobbler

Sweetened buttermilk biscuits crown this summery cobbler infused with lime juice and peel. A sprinkle of coarse sugar before baking gives it crunch and sparkle.

MAKES 8 servings   **PREP** 20 minutes   **BAKE** 40 minutes at 350°F   **STAND** 10 minutes

8	**cups fresh blackberries**
1¼	**cups sugar**
1½	**teaspoons finely shredded lime peel**
2	**tablespoons lime juice**
1	**tablespoon cornstarch**
1¼	**cups all-purpose flour**
1¼	**teaspoons baking powder**
¼	**teaspoon baking soda**
⅛	**teaspoon fine sea salt**
6	**tablespoons unsalted butter, cut into small cubes and chilled**
¼	**cup buttermilk**
	Coarse sugar (optional)

1 Preheat the oven to 350°F.

2 For the blackberry filling, in a large bowl toss together the blackberries, 1 cup of the sugar, and the lime peel. In a small bowl whisk together the lime juice and cornstarch until smooth. Drizzle the lime juice mixture over the blackberries and toss to combine. Transfer filling to a 10-inch cast-iron skillet; set aside.

3 For the biscuit topping, in a medium bowl whisk together the flour, baking powder, baking soda, salt, and the remaining ¼ cup sugar. Use your fingertips to rub the butter into the flour mixture until it is the texture of coarse meal. Make a well in the center of the dry ingredients. Pour the buttermilk into the well and stir with a fork until the dough comes together. Crumble the dough evenly over the top of the blackberry filling. If desired, sprinkle dough with coarse sugar.

4 Bake for 40 to 50 minutes or until the blackberry filling is bubbling and the topping is golden brown. Let cobbler stand 10 minutes before serving.

PER SERVING 341 **CAL**; 24 g **FAT** (6 g **SAT**); 24 mg **CHOL**; 161 mg **SODIUM**; 62 g **CARB**; 8 g **FIBER**; 4 g **PRO**

Cherry Pistachio Crisp

If you use fresh cherries, a cherry pitter is a handy gadget to own. This inexpensive tool is easily found at large retail stores, kitchen stores, and even some hardware stores.

MAKES 10 servings   **PREP** 45 minutes
BAKE 40 minutes at 375°F   **COOL** 30 minutes

2	pounds fresh dark sweet cherries, stemmed and pitted* (about 6 cups)
3	tablespoons granulated sugar
½	teaspoon finely shredded lemon peel
1	tablespoon lemon juice
2	teaspoons cornstarch
¾	cup sliced almonds
½	cup whole wheat pastry flour
½	cup regular rolled oats
½	cup roasted salted pistachio nuts
3	tablespoons packed brown sugar
2	teaspoons baking powder
½	teaspoon baking soda
¼	teaspoon salt
¼	teaspoon ground cinnamon
6	tablespoons cold butter, cut into ½-inch pieces
¼	cup buttermilk

1 Preheat oven to 375°F. Grease a 2-quart rectangular baking dish; set aside. For filling, in a large bowl toss together cherries, granulated sugar, lemon peel, lemon juice, and cornstarch. Spoon into the prepared baking dish; set aside.

2 For topping, place almonds in a food processor. Cover and process until finely ground. Add pastry flour, oats, nuts, brown sugar, baking powder, baking soda, salt, and cinnamon. Pulse until combined. Add butter; pulse until mixture resembles coarse cornmeal. With machine running, add buttermilk through feed tube.

3 Crumble topping evenly over filling in dish. Bake for 40 minutes or until topping is browned and filling is bubbly. Cool in pan on wire rack 30 minutes; serve warm.

*To use frozen cherries, spread 6 cups cherries in a shallow baking pan; thaw at room temperature 30 to 40 minutes or until cherries soften but maintain their shape. Drain, discarding juices.

PER SERVING 260 **CAL**; 14 g **FAT** (5 g **SAT**); 19 mg **CHOL**; 290 mg **SODIUM**; 33 g **CARB**; 4 g **FIBER**; 5 g **PRO**

Chocolate-Walnut Bread Pudding with Coffee-Kahlúa Cream Sauce

To dry the bread, preheat the oven to 300°F. Cut bread into ½-inch cubes. Spread cubes in a shallow baking pan. Bake 10 to 15 minutes, stirring twice, until dried; cool completely before using.

MAKES 12 servings   **PREP** 20 minutes
BAKE 50 minutes at 350°F

6	cups dried French bread cubes
1¼	cups semisweet chocolate pieces
1	cup coarsely chopped walnuts
4	eggs, lightly beaten
3	cups milk
1	cup sugar
1	tablespoon vanilla
1	recipe Coffee-Kahlúa Cream Sauce

1 Preheat oven to 350°F. Generously grease a 3-quart rectangular baking dish. Spread bread cubes in the prepared baking dish. Sprinkle with chocolate pieces and walnuts.

2 In a large bowl combine eggs, milk, sugar, and vanilla. Pour egg mixture evenly over bread mixture. Using the back of a large spoon, gently press down on bread mixture to moisten.

3 Bake for 50 to 60 minutes or until a knife inserted near the center comes out clean. If necessary to prevent overbrowning, cover loosely with foil the last 5 to 10 minutes of baking. Cool slightly. Serve warm with Coffee-Kahlúa Cream Sauce.

Coffee-Kahlúa Cream Sauce In a medium saucepan stir together ½ cup sugar and 4 teaspoons cornstarch. Add 1 cup whipping cream, ½ cup freshly brewed strong coffee, and Kahlúa or other coffee liqueur or water. Cook and stir over medium heat until thickened and bubbly. Cook and stir for 2 minutes more.

PER SERVING 455 **CAL**; 22 g **FAT** (9 g **SAT**); 103 mg **CHOL**; 175 mg **SODIUM**; 56 g **CARB**; 2 g **FIBER**; 9 g **PRO**

CHOCOLATE-WALNUT BREAD
PUDDING WITH COFFEE-KAHLÚA
CREAM SAUCE

Bourbon Brownies

Bourbon and pecans give these decadent brownies a Southern accent.

MAKES 16 servings   **PREP** 35 minutes   **BAKE** 25 minutes at 350°F

½ **cup granulated sugar**
⅓ **cup butter**
2 **tablespoons water**
1 **cup semisweet chocolate pieces**
2 **eggs**
1 **teaspoon vanilla**
¾ **cup all-purpose flour**
¼ **teaspoon baking soda**
¼ **teaspoon salt**
½ **cup chopped pecans, toasted (see tip, page 47)**
2 **to 3 tablespoons bourbon**
1 **recipe Bourbon Frosting**
2 **ounces semisweet chocolate, melted**
   Pecan halves, toasted (see tip, page 47) (optional)

1 Preheat oven to 350°F. Grease an 8×8×2-inch baking pan; set aside. In a medium saucepan combine sugar, butter, and the water. Stir over medium heat just until boiling. Remove from heat.

2 Stir in 1 cup chocolate pieces until melted. Add eggs and vanilla, beating with a wooden spoon just until combined. Stir in flour, baking soda, and salt. Stir in chopped pecans. Pour batter into the prepared pan, spreading evenly.

3 Bake for 25 minutes or until a wooden toothpick inserted near center comes out clean and edges start to pull away from sides of pan.

4 Place pan on a wire rack. Brush top of hot brownies with bourbon. Cool completely on rack.

5 Spread brownies with Bourbon Frosting. Cut into bars. Top each with some of the melted chocolate and, if desired, a pecan half.

Bourbon Frosting In a medium bowl beat 3 tablespoons softened butter with a mixer on medium to high for 30 seconds. Gradually add 1½ cups powdered sugar, beating well. Beat in 1 to 2 tablespoons bourbon or milk and ¼ teaspoon vanilla. If necessary, beat in enough milk, 1 teaspoon at a time, to make a frosting of spreading consistency.

PER SERVING 235 **CAL**; 13 g **FAT** (6 g **SAT**); 44 mg **CHOL**; 129 mg **SODIUM**; 24 g **CARB**; 2 g **FIBER**; 2 g **PRO**

Brownie Waffles à la Mode

During the holiday season, look for peppermint ice cream in the freezer section of your supermarket. Substitute it for the vanilla ice cream mixed with crushed peppermint candies, if you like.

MAKES 10 servings   **PREP** 40 minutes   **FREEZE** 8 hours   **COOK** according to manufacturer's directions

1	quart vanilla ice cream
½	cup crushed striped round peppermint candies*
2	ounces unsweetened chocolate, chopped
¼	cup butter
½	cup all-purpose flour
¼	cup unsweetened cocoa powder
¼	teaspoon baking powder
¼	teaspoon baking soda
¼	teaspoon salt
2	eggs, lightly beaten
⅔	cup sugar
¼	cup half-and-half or light cream
1	teaspoon vanilla
½	teaspoon instant espresso coffee powder (optional)
	Nonstick cooking spray
	Chocolate fudge ice cream topping
	Crushed striped round peppermint candies (optional)

1 In a large chilled bowl combine ice cream and ½ cup crushed candies. Stir with a wooden spoon just until combined. Cover and freeze about 8 hours or until firm.

2 In a small saucepan stir unsweetened chocolate and butter over low heat until melted; cool.

3 In a medium bowl stir together flour, cocoa powder, baking powder, baking soda, and salt. Make a well in the center of flour mixture. In a small bowl combine eggs, sugar, half-and-half, vanilla, espresso powder (if desired), and cooled melted chocolate mixture. Add egg mixture all at once to flour mixture. Stir just until moistened (batter should be slightly lumpy).

4 Preheat a 7½-inch round waffle baker; lightly coat surface with cooking spray. Spoon a scant ½ cup of the batter onto grids of preheated waffle baker. Close lid quickly; do not open until done. Bake according to manufacturer's directions. (Waffle will not be crisp; do not overcook). When done, use a fork to lift waffle off grid. Cool on a wire rack. Repeat with the remaining batter.

5 Separate waffles into quarters. Serve waffle sections and ice cream in dessert dishes. Drizzle with fudge topping and, if desired, sprinkle with additional crushed candies.

* If desired, omit the peppermint candies and use coffee, butter pecan, or strawberry premium ice cream.

PER SERVING 396 **CAL**; 21 g **FAT** (12 g **SAT**); 113 mg **CHOL**; 313 mg **SODIUM**; 49 g **CARB**; 1 g **FIBER**; 6 g **PRO**

Lemony Glazed Shortbread Bars

The beauty of shortbread is that its simplicity allows the flavor of butter to really shine. If shortbread can be improved upon, surely a touch of refreshing lemon is the trick.

MAKES 32 servings **PREP** 40 minutes **BAKE** 40 minutes at 300°F

- **3** **cups all-purpose flour**
- **⅓** **cup cornstarch**
- **1¼** **cups powdered sugar**
- **¼** **cup finely shredded lemon peel (5 to 6 lemons)**
- **1½** **cups butter, softened**
- **1** **tablespoon lemon juice**
- **½** **teaspoon salt**
- **½** **teaspoon vanilla**
- **1** **recipe Lemony Glaze**

1 Preheat oven to 300°F. Line a 13×9×2-inch baking pan with foil, extending the foil over edges of pan. Lightly grease foil; set pan aside.

2 In a medium bowl stir together flour and cornstarch; set aside. In a small bowl combine powdered sugar and lemon peel. Pressing against side of bowl with a wooden spoon, work lemon peel into powdered sugar until sugar is yellow and fragrant; set aside.

3 In a large mixing bowl beat butter, lemon juice, salt, and vanilla with a mixer on medium until combined. Gradually beat in sugar mixture. Stir in flour mixture.

4 Using lightly floured fingers, evenly press dough into the prepared baking pan. Bake for 40 minutes or until lightly browned and edges start to brown. Remove from oven.

5 Immediately spoon Lemony Glaze over top, spreading gently to edges. Cool in pan on a wire rack. Using the edges of the foil, lift uncut bars out of pan. Cut into bars.

Lemony Glaze In a bowl combine 2½ cups powdered sugar, 2 teaspoons finely shredded lemon peel, 3 tablespoons lemon juice, 1 teaspoon light-color corn syrup, and ½ teaspoon vanilla. Whisk until smooth.

PER SERVING 181 **CAL**; 9 g **FAT** (5 g **SAT**); 23 mg **CHOL**; 98 mg **SODIUM**; 25 g **CARB**; 1 g **PRO**

SALTED CHOCOLATE-
CARAMEL ROUNDS

Salted Chocolate-Caramel Rounds

Use flaked sea salt—such as Maldon—to top these tender cookies.

MAKES 8 servings   **PREP** 30 minutes
BAKE 8 minutes at 375°F

2¾ cups all-purpose flour
¾ cup unsweetened cocoa powder
1 teaspoon baking soda
¼ teaspoon salt
1 cup butter, softened
1 cup granulated sugar
1 cup packed brown sugar
2 eggs
2 teaspoons vanilla
36 milk chocolate-covered round caramels
12 vanilla caramels, unwrapped
1 tablespoon whipping cream, half-and-half, or light cream
   Coarse salt

1 In a medium bowl stir together flour, cocoa powder, baking soda, and salt; set aside.

2 In a large bowl beat butter with a mixer on medium to high for 30 seconds. Add granulated and brown sugars. Beat until combined, scraping sides of bowl occasionally. Beat in eggs and vanilla until combined. Beat in as much of the flour mixture as you can with the mixer. Stir in any remaining flour mixture. If necessary, cover and chill for 1 hour or until dough is easy to handle.

3 Preheat oven to 375°F. Shape dough into 1½-inch balls. Press a chocolate-covered caramel into each ball and shape dough around caramel to enclose. Place cookies 2 inches apart on an ungreased cookie sheet.

4 Bake for 8 to 10 minutes or until edges are firm. Transfer cookies to a wire rack; cool.

5 For caramel drizzle, in a small saucepan combine vanilla caramels and whipping cream. Melt and stir over medium-low heat until mixture is smooth. Drizzle melted caramel over cookies then sprinkle cookies with coarse salt. Let stand until set.

PER SERVING 177 **CAL**; 8 g **FAT** (5 g **SAT**); 27 mg **CHOL**; 140 mg **SODIUM**; 26 g **CARB**; 1 g **FIBER**; 2 g **PRO**

Praline Snickerdoodles

Toffee pieces and chopped pecans add flavor and texture to these cinnamon-sugar coated cookies.

MAKES 48 servings   **PREP** 30 minutes   **CHILL** 1 hour
BAKE 10 minutes at 375°F

1 cup butter, softened
1¾ cups sugar
1 teaspoon cream of tartar
1 teaspoon baking soda
¼ teaspoon salt
2 eggs
1 teaspoon vanilla
3 cups all-purpose flour
1 cup toffee pieces
½ cup chopped pecans
2 teaspoons ground cinnamon

1 In a large mixing bowl beat butter with a mixer on medium to high for 30 seconds. Add 1½ cups of the sugar, the cream of tartar, baking soda, and salt. Beat until combined, scraping sides of bowl occasionally. Beat in eggs and vanilla until combined. Beat in as much of the flour as you can with the mixer. Using a wooden spoon, stir in any remaining flour, the toffee pieces, and pecans. Cover and chill about 1 hour or until dough is easy to handle.

2 Preheat oven to 375°F. In a small bowl stir together the remaining ¼ cup sugar and cinnamon. Shape dough into 1½-inch balls. Roll balls in cinnamon-sugar to coat.

3 Place balls 2 inches apart on an ungreased cookie sheet. Bake for 10 to 12 minutes or until edges are golden. Transfer cookies to a wire rack; cool.

PER SERVING 126 **CAL**; 6 g **FAT** (3 g **SAT**); 22 mg **CHOL**; 89 mg **SODIUM**; 16 g **CARB**; 1 g **PRO**

Index

Metric Information

The charts on this page provide a guide for converting measurements from the U.S. customary system, which is used throughout this book, to the metric system.

PRODUCT DIFFERENCES

Most of the ingredients called for in the recipes in this book are available in most countries. However, some are known by different names. Here are some common American ingredients and their possible counterparts:

- Sugar (white) is granulated, fine granulated, or castor sugar.
- Confectioners' sugar is icing sugar.
- All-purpose flour is enriched, bleached or unbleached white household flour. When self-rising flour is used in place of all-purpose flour in a recipe that calls for leavening, omit the leavening agent (baking soda or baking powder) and salt.
- Light-color corn syrup is golden syrup.
- Cornstarch is cornflour.
- Baking soda is bicarbonate of soda.
- Vanilla or vanilla extract is vanilla essence.
- Green, red, or yellow sweet peppers are capsicums or bell peppers.
- Golden raisins are sultanas.

VOLUME AND WEIGHT

The United States traditionally uses cup measures for liquid and solid ingredients. The chart, top right, shows the approximate imperial and metric equivalents. If you are accustomed to weighing solid ingredients, the following approximate equivalents will be helpful.

- 1 cup butter, castor sugar, or rice = 8 ounces = ½ pound = 250 grams
- 1 cup flour = 4 ounces = ¼ pound = 125 grams
- 1 cup icing sugar = 5 ounces = 150 grams

Canadian and U.S. volume for a cup measure is 8 fluid ounces (237 ml), but the standard metric equivalent is 250 ml.

1 British imperial cup is 10 fluid ounces.

In Australia, 1 tablespoon equals 20 ml, and there are 4 teaspoons in the Australian tablespoon.

Spoon measures are used for smaller amounts of ingredients. Although the size of the tablespoon varies slightly in different countries, for practical purposes and for recipes in this book, a straight substitution is all that's necessary. Measurements made using cups or spoons should always be level unless stated otherwise.

COMMON WEIGHT RANGE REPLACEMENTS

Imperial/U.S.	Metric
½ ounce	15 g
1 ounce	25 g or 30 g
4 ounces (¼ pound)	115 g or 125 g
8 ounces (½ pound)	225 g or 250 g
16 ounces (1 pound)	450 g or 500 g
1¼ pounds	625 g
1½ pounds	750 g
2 pounds or 2¼ pounds	1,000 g or 1 Kg

OVEN TEMPERATURE EQUIVALENTS

Fahrenheit Setting	Celsius Setting*	Gas Setting
300°F	150°C	Gas Mark 2 (very low)
325°F	160°C	Gas Mark 3 (low)
350°F	180°C	Gas Mark 4 (moderate)
375°F	190°C	Gas Mark 5 (moderate)
400°F	200°C	Gas Mark 6 (hot)
425°F	220°C	Gas Mark 7 (hot)
450°F	230°C	Gas Mark 8 (very hot)
475°F	240°C	Gas Mark 9 (very hot)
500°F	260°C	Gas Mark 10 (extremely hot)
Broil	Broil	Grill

*Electric and gas ovens may be calibrated using celsius. However, for an electric oven, increase celsius setting 10 to 20 degrees when cooking above 160°C. For convection or forced air ovens (gas or electric) lower the temperature setting 25°F/10°C when cooking at all heat levels.

BAKING PAN SIZES

Imperial/U.S.	Metric
9x1½-inch round cake pan	22- or 23x4-cm (1.5 L)
9x1½-inch pie plate	22- or 23x4-cm (1 L)
8x8x2-inch square cake pan	20x5-cm (2 L)
9x9x2-inch square cake pan	22- or 23x4.5-cm (2.5 L)
11x7x1½-inch baking pan	28x17x4-cm (2 L)
2-quart rectangular baking pan	30x19x4.5-cm (3 L)
13x9x2-inch baking pan	34x22x4.5-cm (3.5 L)
15x10x1-inch jelly roll pan	40x25x2-cm
9x5x3-inch loaf pan	23x13x8-cm (2 L)
2-quart casserole	2 L

U.S./STANDARD METRIC EQUIVALENTS

⅛ teaspoon = 0.5 ml	⅓ cup = 3 fluid ounces = 75 ml
¼ teaspoon = 1 ml	½ cup = 4 fluid ounces = 125 ml
½ teaspoon = 2 ml	⅔ cup = 5 fluid ounces = 150 ml
1 teaspoon = 5 ml	¾ cup = 6 fluid ounces = 175 ml
1 tablespoon = 15 ml	1 cup = 8 fluid ounces = 250 ml
2 tablespoons = 25 ml	2 cups = 1 pint = 500 ml
¼ cup = 2 fluid ounces = 50 ml	1 quart = 1 litre